VETS

50 PORTRAITS OF VETERANS AND THEIR STORIES

John Thamm

Stories by Tom I. Davis   Edited by Ruth Danner

Gray Dog Press
Spokane, Washington
www.GrayDogPress.com

ISBN: 978-1-936178-26-1

Edited by Ruth Danner
Stories by Tom I. Davis unless otherwise noted

DEDICATION

This book is dedicated to my daughter Amy Thamm, November 24, 1968 ~ March 8, 2009, and all those veterans out there who have taken their own lives and those who are considering it. Please don't do it.

John Thamm

ACKNOWLEDGEMENTS

I would like to thank Tom Davis for his help in conducting the veteran interviews and writing the drafts from the transcriptions. His encouragement and enthusiasm for this project and his sincere interest in each of the veterans carried me through the difficult times in the process.

Thanks also go to Russ Davis, the owner of Gray Dog Press, Paul Quinnett, Dick Bresgal, Karen Allen, Judith Davis and Olivia Wegis contributing writers; Desiree Doyle who transcribed over 70 hours of interviews; Ruth Danner, editor; Sharon Helman, Chuck Marsden, Dianna Bradley, Kevin Bratcher and Carsten Michelson at the Spokane Veterans Medical Center for their support of the project and love of the veterans; Jill Johnson, producer and Dan Jackson, photographer KSPS NorthWest Profiles; Heather Thamm, my daughter the photographer who offered me continual support; brother-in-law Ron Decker for his advice; and my wife, Kathy Thamm who supported the writing, editing, blogging, book design and show installation of the fifty portraits.

I would also like to thank the fifty veterans for their patience and perseverance through the phases of this book. Their stories changed my life.

FOREWORD

One day two years ago I came across a letter to the editor in the Spokesman Review, the one and only Spokane daily paper. It was a letter from a VA volunteer appealing for more volunteers to assist at the Spokane Veterans Hospital. Not wanting to drive the bus or golf cart, I decided I'd paint portraits of some of the patients out there. Little did I know then that this book would be the result and the length of time and effort which it would take to produce it. I will describe the evolution of the project.

Originally I thought I'd just go out there, set up an easel and my paints, and, hopefully, find some good subject matter . . . which I did. Watching me do my thing seemed to ease the tedium and boredom suffered by these veterans who I met while waiting for their appointments. After talking to them I began to realize the importance of their individual stories and how their unimaginable experiences had shaped their lives. So I began to see this project in a different way. Their stories became equally important as the pictures I was painting. My poet friend Tom Davis then got involved and we decided to put the materials into book form. Tom and I would interview the veterans, transcribe the interviews, and then turn them into story form.

I decided to divide the book into several sections: WWII, Korea, Viet Nam, and a few from our latest conflicts. Not all the stories were tragic. Some veterans escaped the misery of PTSD, agent orange, shrapnel, and physical devastation. The dividing line seemed to be combat. I decided to include a dozen of my closest friends most of whom like myself did their duty and didn't suffer from the experience. We were lucky since our service fell between Korea and Vietnam.

The veterans of WWII that I interviewed felt they were involved in a just war: "We kicked the Japs' and the Krauts' ass and lived to tell about it." They are in their 80's and 90's now, and psychologically in much better shape than those who saw combat in later wars. Some told me "We just sucked it up and went on with life as best we could."

Korea was a different story. Some expressed their bitterness about being involved in what was called "A United Nations Policing Action." One vet told me " it was a hot war that couldn't get any hotter and fought for the most part by the United States."

Then came Viet Nam. Some joined up for the adventure and some were conscripted. "Some gave some and some gave all." "This conflict dragged on endlessly and eventually was lost by the politicians." One veteran told me it wasn't lost; "Vietnam is now a trading partner with the U.S. Therefore we did win." But at what price? There was the inevitable racial conflict inside the military coupled with the question: "War, war, what are we fighting for?" Or another Vet said, "Slip on their moccasins (the Vietnamese) for a moment. What would you do if your country was invaded?" These interviews revealed fragging incidents, insubordination, and out right hostility for some of those who had to fight the war. Some of the interviews focused on the humiliation that they experienced when they came home from Vietnam listening to the cries of "Baby Killer" by the anti-war protesters. One veteran's recent observation was: "Hardly enough time has passed to heal up from one conflict before we are into another one."

The art show at the VA Medical Center of the 50 veteran portraits for this book was one of the major high points for me. Many of these veterans came to the opening with their families and asked to have their pictures taken with their portraits and me. I've heard over and over again how much the recognition meant to them, their families and friends. This show was a true morale booster for all concerned. The director of the Spokane VA, Sharon Helman, was there and spoke to the benefits these veterans experienced.

In July 2009 Spokane hosted the "Wheel Chair Events". The Spokane VA commissioned me to do a painting of Brent King, one of the participants in the wheel chair event. I was honored that the VA presented the painting to Secretary Shinseki at that time.

I feel good about what I've done. This project was unique. It gives me satisfaction to know the veterans appreciated the recognition that they received.

John Thamm

INTRODUCTION TO VETS
Paul Quinnett

I was–am–a soldier.

I say "am" because once you have been a soldier, you may become many things, but you will always be a soldier.

Like the men and women you will meet in this book, my life may have been shaped by my parents, my religion, my teachers, and my friends, but it was transformed by a short, strong, bespectacled man from Puerto Rico; my DI in boot camp. His business was turning boys into men and for his "tough love" I will be forever grateful.

It was only after slowly pouring through this remarkable collection of portraits and personal stories in *Vets* that I realized why there is this connection, this brotherhood, this sense of automatic bonding with other veterans that makes being a veteran something special. We may have served in different eras, in different services, in different units, in different countries, in combat or not in combat, in a hot war or a cold one, but the bond somehow holds us together.

Because of the men and women you will meet in *Vets* I am honored to write this introduction. I stand in awe of the things that these veterans have seen and done, lived through, endured, survived and, yes, even conquered.

I wish I knew each of them personally.

I think you will, too.

If you are a veteran as you read these stories, you will find yourself nodding, smiling, and, perhaps, cheering inside, or tearing up.

Sometimes you will feel the way you do now when taps are played at sundown.

Sometimes you will feel yourself marching once more; strong, in perfect time with the cadence caller, stepping together in unison with your squad or company or regiment while pounding down the parade ground in that smooth, well-oiled machine known as a "fighting unit."

If you are not a veteran, you will still find the sense of pride and connectedness that runs through these stories and, perhaps, to friends and loved ones in your own life. History shows that not every war proves a popular or just one, and that those who chose to help end a war by not fighting in it, also served in a just cause greater than themselves.

Soldiering causes a lasting mark not just on how we walk and hold our bodies, but on our very souls; it changes us in ways we never imagined possible, and makes possible things we never imagined.

If I may indulge the reader just a bit, as I read these stories and studied these faces, I felt a rush of old connections, old stories, family histories, personal memories and experiences that seemed to weave us— everyone in *Vets*—together into a rich, whole cloth of lives spent in parallel passage to the same places.

In the portraits I saw the faces of my father, my uncles, my brothers, and my brothers-in-arms—all veterans, all of them having once been a part of something bigger than themselves.

In one *Vets* story a man had fought in General Patton's 3rd Army in Italy and beyond. One of my uncles—one I never met—fought in Italy and was killed there in World War II. I never learned if he was in Patton's Army, but he might have been.

My college roommate was John Waters, III, son of General John Waters, son-in-law of General George Patton, the same Lt. Colonel Waters who was captured by Rommel's forces in North Africa in 1942 and later rescued by Patton from a German POW camp on his race through Europe.

After his retirement, John's General-of-the-Army father, now deceased, came to Utah State University to visit his son. He took us out to a fine dinner, but on the way asked if we would like to shoot one of Patton's famous ivory handled pistols. We said "sure!" and so we drove up Logan Canyon, found a safe place to plink, and took turns blasting beer cans with one of the General's famous .45s—a recreation I doubt old Blood and Guts would have greeted with much approval.

My father told Patton stories and handed down some snapshots of him that he (or someone) took in North Africa in early 1943 after volunteering for the civilian side of the Army Air Corps (Dad had too many children to enlist in the regular Army, but wanted to get in the fight). As you will read in *Vets*, other soldiers have Patton stories to tell. In this way we are "connected."

Other connections...

My uncle Addison, a Navy man, served as the harbormaster in Guam during WW II. My uncle Norv, Army Air Force, flew transports from Burma into China and once piloted General MacArthur over "The Hump" of the Himalayas to an inland Chinese base. He said at a campfire one night, "Nobody liked the son-of-bitch and I didn't either, so I gave him a rough ride."

The *Vets* stories from the Cold War and Viet Nam hooked me deeply, as my request to transfer to Viet Nam in 1963 (before we knew there was going to be a shooting war), reminded me that luck plays a big part in our lives, and that it cuts both ways, good and bad, and especially in the life of a soldier.

It was good luck for me because at the last minute after my orders had been cut, the brass decided to send Marines with my MOS first into Viet Nam instead of the Army. But it was bad luck that my younger brother, Jim, spent 1968 in combat in Viet Nam. But then it was good luck again that Jim was one of the few guys in his outfit not killed or wounded and made it home, if not at peace in his mind, at least in one piece. And it was good luck that my older brother, John, US Army, was sent to fight the Cold War in Germany where, he claims, the only bad luck was to draw the short straw and have to pay for the beer.

The connections just keep running for me, and I believe when you read *Vets* the connections will run for you, too.

A final note...

The stories in *Vets* are about men and women mostly from the Spokane area, from the Inland Northwest. But if you were to gather together 50 veterans from Dallas or Miami or San Bernardino or Albuquerque or

Fargo or Birmingham or New York City, the names and faces might change, but the stories would ring just as true as these.

You would find all the same threads and themes that make us what we are as men and women connected together in military service to our nation, and as Americans. Some of us volunteered, some of us were drafted, and some of us chose to enlist to avoid being drafted, and some of us signed up just for the hell of it. But one way or another we all served our country.

You will also find that John Thamm has dedicated *Vets* to those who have died by suicide and to those thinking about suicide in the hopes they will not do it. Perhaps it was more good luck that the G.I. Bill allowed me to earn a Ph.D. in Clinical Psychology so that I could, for much of my career, devote my professional life and work to the prevention of suicide not only among our active military and veterans, but to those suffering unbearable psychological pain around the world.

In my seventh decade as I write this, I vividly remember the night America and its allies invaded Iraq to right the wrongs done to the people of Kuwait by Saddam Hussein.

After watching our troops on TV enter into the breach that makes and seals the peace for others, and while the battle raged, I took a long walk with my Labrador retriever in the still of the evening through the quiet woods around my home. Just between you and me, I wept just a bit that I was now too old to get into the fight.

As I said, I was—and am—a soldier.

Paul Quinnett
Cheney, Washington
US Army 1960-1963.
February 19, 2010

Paul Quinnett's background as a clinical psychologist allowed him to write an excellent book on suicide prevention titled *The Forever Decision* and can be found on the internet when searching for the title. This book is used extensively by the Veterans Administration.

WORLD WAR II

KOREA

COLD WAR

VIETNAM

POST VIETNAM

DESERT STORM

IRAQ

World War II

VERNON BAKER
First Lieutenant
US ARMY AIRBORNE

World War II

VERNON BAKER
St. Maries, Idaho

I am haunted by the memory of nineteen men; men I left on a ridge in northern Italy five decades ago.

I still hear a German commander scream "Feuer," howitzer shells whistling in, followed by the whish, whish, whish of mortars, the trees around us shredding. Wounded and dying men screaming. My only medic killed by a sniper as we try to withdraw.

A film of burned cordite covers the roof of my mouth and cottons my tongue. It's April 1945 in Italy's Northern Apennine Mountains and my men and I have been trading bullets and grenades with the German Army for so long that the air is more spent powder than oxygen. I know, as soon as this taste bites my tongue, the images will follow.

I gather dog tags from my dead comrades, time after time, figuring their bodies probably never will be recovered, that their families deserve to know where and when they died. I see the living wrestle rifles and ammunition from the dead and mortally wounded, taking from those who have given everything, so the rest of us can live and fight a little longer.

I hear, over and over again, my company commander telling me he is going for reinforcements. I stare long and hard at Captain John F. Runyon as he gives me that story. He trudges away, disappearing forever into the late morning haze, the haze of exploding shells, bodies, and blood. Yet today, I cannot remember a detail from his face, except that it was a white man's face, whiter yet, nearly translucent, with fear.

Blame? Rage? Perhaps. I am angry and aghast that he never returned. But more likely this memory lapse is habit. There was no reason to memorize anything distinguishing about Runyon or any other white commander. A white officer in charge of black troops could ask to be relieved of his command at any time and that wish had to be granted immediately.

The rest of us were black Buffalo Soldiers, regarded as too worthless to lead ourselves. The Army decided we needed supervision from white Southerners, as if war was plantation work and fighting Germans was picking cotton.

Harsh as those words seem, I can't work up much bitterness anymore. Yet, I cannot forget the faces of the men who died beside me, nor can I stop wondering if, as their platoon leader, I am responsible for their deaths.

I am haunted by what I cannot remember. Everywhere I go, people ask me to recite the names of those nineteen men I left in the shadow of Castle Aghinolfi. No doubt studio audiences and readers would be more satisfied if I could give dramatic discourse about how several men, closer to me than brothers, died agonizing but glorious deaths, imbued with heroism that stirs God Bless America in every soul.

Continued on page 114

ARCHIE STALEY
First Lieutenant
US ARMY AIR FORCE

World War II

ARCHIE STALEY
Medical Lake, Washington

"We followed a pattern for the work ethics of man: the mind perceives,
the heart believes and the hands achieve." -- Archie Staley

Growing up in Washtucna, Washington, Archie Staley worked hard in the wheat fields. One of his main occupations as a farm hand involved controlling the number of wild animals destructive to the crop and livestock. He targeted jackrabbits, ground squirrels and coyotes with his 44-40 Winchester.

Such experiences helped him develop a sense of responsibility. In addition, he proved to be an excellent student at Washtucna School, where he graduated in 1938 as valedictorian. He received a scholarship to Whitman College in Walla Walla, and he studied for 2-1/2 years to become a teacher.

But two occurrences forced him to change his plans.

In December 1941, Archie's mother became seriously ill. The doctors agreed that nothing could be done for her. In response, her son refused to go back to college at the end of that semester. He stayed home, got a job and helped his family with finances.

This led to the second occurrence. No longer a student, Archie discovered his name went to the draft board, and soon he received his notice. His mother died in March 1942, and Archie left for USAAF training four months later.

Archie's academic and physical abilities allowed him to advance quickly. He took pre-flight training and graduated from pilots' school in October 1943.

Upon receiving his commission and his wings, Archie took a ten-day leave, visiting Alene Gillis, his high-school sweetheart, in Spokane, Washington. When he proposed to her, she accepted, and he pinned a set of wings on her jacket. He then headed to Florida on the troop train for his next phase of training.

The young pilot and Alene arranged to meet in Florida and were married in February 1944. Archie left for Europe the following July. His flight crew traveled from Langley Field, Virginia, to the west coast of Africa below Casablanca at Marrakech.

From Marrakech they flew to Tunis, where the allies had just captured Rommel and his artillery. "The artillery and leftover ammo was bulldozed into piles about eight feet high," Archie recalls. "I'm not sure what happened to all of it, but there sure was a lot of it. There were mines and explosive traps planted all over the place, so we weren't allowed to wander in Tunis." Each man got two blankets and slept on the ground. In case of rain, they camped out under the wing of their B-17.

The crew left Tunis to fly corridor because Italy was not yet cleared of the enemy. "Flying corridor" indicates travel along a designated pathway to avoid anti-aircraft attacks. They flew corridor to Bari, Italy. From there the crew went inland to Lucera, about 12 miles north of Foggia, where they joined the 32nd Squadron of the 301st Bomber Group, in late July 1944.

Continued on page 115

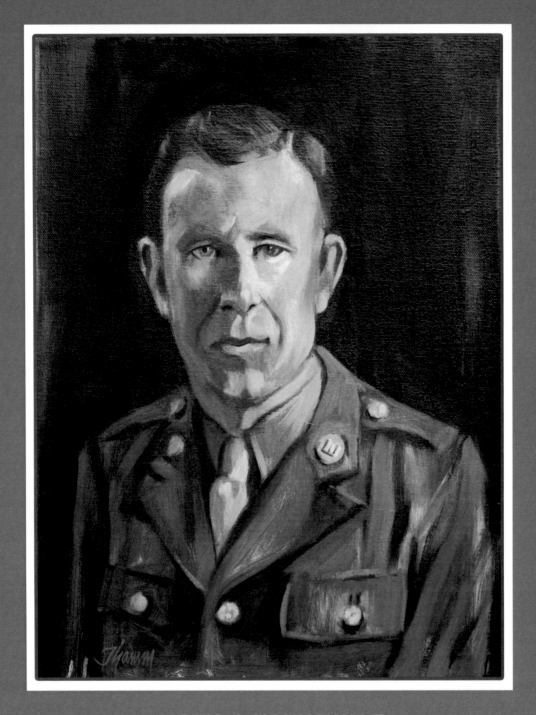

JAMES J. HANNAWALT
E-6
US ARMY CORPS of ENGINEERS

1906 ~ 1977

World War II

JAMES J. HANNAWALT
Spokane, Washington

In 1941 James Hannawalt should not have been drafted. He was 36 years old, married with two children. But, as his daughter Mary Joyce Kiphart explains in retrospect, "The lady who ran the draft board didn't like my mom, so my dad got a draft notice."

He joined the Army Corps of Engineers and became a platoon sergeant. Even though he started out as a cook, his superiors soon discovered he had a variety of skills, and they moved him into an engineering unit at McCord.

From there he was sent to Europe, landing on the beach of Normandy 48 hours after D-Day. Immediately he began working to build runways on the hill above the beaches. Mary Joyce recalls her father's account: "It rained so hard we couldn't mix concrete. So we laid out metal mesh mats. We just rolled them out in the mud and poured the dry concrete on top of them. They became one of the hardest runways we'd ever constructed."

Eventually Hannawalt reached the rank of E6-Technical Sergeant. Mary Joyce says, "He used to tell stories about the lieutenants that didn't see eye-to-eye with him, and how his colonel said he'd swap one CO for 100 lieutenants."

After his discharge, he rejoined his family in the Spokane area and worked at the Millwood paper mill. Always handy with tools, he collected pieces of leftover lumber, with his supervisor's permission, and used it to build a patio at his home. He even added rooms to the house to accommodate his growing family, which eventually numbered six children.

Sadly, James lost an eye in an accident at the paper mill. But Mary Joyce says the resulting VA disability pension helped the family. In his last years, he suffered several strokes, requiring months of recuperation. "But the VA took really good care of him," says his daughter.

Mary Joyce remembers her father as a quiet, handsome man, protective of his children—especially his two girls. When Mary Joyce herself considered a career in the military, James balked at first. But, she says, she joined the Air Force anyway.

"When I made E5, he was pretty proud."

Good Conduct Medal

C. BENNETT CROWLEY
Private
US ARMY

1916 ~ 2008

World War II

C. BENNETT CROWLEY
Spokane, Washington

On the Fourth of July in 1916, Charles Crowley almost killed his mother. But the deed wouldn't have been intentional. As a nine-pound baby, he caused her a difficult birthing. However, the boy made restitution in the years that followed by helping to support the family, getting an education and finishing college with a major in business.

When friend Horus Bergman was drafted in 1942, Crowley followed by enlisting in Butte, Montana. He shipped out to Trowbridge Barracks in England within a year.

In June 1944 he arrived at Normandy Beach, a week after D-Day. Joining the 7th Unit of the 21st Division in Paris, he made his way toward Colmar, France, where he fought in January and February 1945. During this period he witnessed the death of PFC Jose F. Valdez, who sacrificed himself near Rosenkranz to cover the withdrawal of other members of his squad and was posthumously awarded the Medal of Honor.

Once the Colmar pocket was closed, the 7th Unit headed to the Saar Basin of Germany, meeting the 3rd Division led by General Patton. From there they moved northeast, reaching the Rhine River on March 22, 1945. They made a brief stop—long enough for General Patton to take his famous piss in the river.

In early May, Germany officially surrendered, and Crowley's unit accepted the challenge of rebuilding postwar Europe. On their way to Austria, they came upon a camp on the outskirts of the small town of Ebensee. When the American soldiers opened the door to a large warehouse on the compound, the sights and sounds and smells they experienced would never be forgotten.

Inside languished some 16,000 prisoners of war.[1]

Crowley soon discovered these prisoners had little food and had been dying at the rate of 400 per day. Until the Red Cross could arrive, the 3rd Unit did their best to nurture the prisoners. Unfortunately, many died of hunger, disease and exhaustion despite the Americans' best efforts.

Even though the war was over, Crowley and his fellow soldiers still had work to do. After being relieved of their work in Ebensee, they traveled to Africa and trained for possible deployment to Japan. However, since Japan surrendered near the end of that summer, Crowley was soon discharged. He returned home in January 1946 with no injuries and two Bronze Stars.

Continued on page 116

---

[1] The Ebensee concentration camp was known for its inhumane working and living conditions. It was one of the worst Nazi concentration camps for the death rates of its prisoners. The SS used several codenames, like Kalk (*limestone*), Kalksteinbergwerk (*limestone mine*), Solvay and Zement (*cement*), to conceal the true nature of the camp. The main purpose of Ebensee was to provide slave labor for the construction of enormous underground tunnels in which armament works were to be housed. But on July 6, 1944, Hitler ordered the complex converted to a tank-gear factory. Jews formed about one third of the inmates, a percentage which increased to 40% by the end of the war, and were the worst treated, though all inmates suffered great hardships.

FRANK R. MACE
Chaplain
US NAVY / P.O.W.

World War II

FRANK R. MACE
Cheney, Washington

Adapted from his book, The Story of Wake Island:
Before, During and After Life as a Prisoner of War of the Japanese for 44 Months

Growing up in the '20s and '30s on a dairy farm in eastern Washington, Frank Mace milked cows every morning before heading off to school on his spotted donkey. After all, there were no school busses in those days.

Besides chores and studying, he stayed busy with sports, including football and basketball. But another sport claimed first place in his life. "I lived to play baseball," he says, "and had a .413 batting average with lots of home runs." After high school, he met a baseball scout, who asked him to try out for the Seattle Rainiers.

They made the trip over the Cascades and onto a practice field. "The manager said to get a bat, and he went out to the pitcher and told him to throw everything he had," Mace remembers. "Each baseball that came over the plate was in the strike zone. I drove them out of the ball park." To his delight, the team offered him a contract for $250 per month, plus room and board. He played a season with Seattle and another with the Wenatchee Chiefs.

But baseball would not be Mace's lifelong career. He eventually became a carpenter foreman for Morrison Knutson and Company of Boise, Idaho, on Wake Island. He was transferred to the island, arriving there on January 9, 1941. "I was there eleven months before the War started." December 8, 1941, he learned that the Japanese had bombed Pearl Harbor.

He notes, "The Japanese held the Marshall Islands and needed Wake Island for a refueling place for their ships and planes." The Japanese launched 36 bombers in a surprise attack on Wake. They destroyed eight fighter planes on the ground, bombed and destroyed the Pan Air Hotel and fired on a military camp. That day Mace was conscripted into the Marines and later the Navy to help defend the island.

The next day brought more of the same. Twenty-seven Japanese bombers demolished the hospital, and by December 11, five Japanese naval vessels were sighted off the island. Mace recalls the period from December 12 to 23, when Wake Island suffered daily attacks from the enemy. Over fifty ships surrounded the island.

Finally the Americans surrendered, and Frank became a prisoner of war. "All the men remained concentrated at the airport under heavy guard," he says of the prisoners. "We slept on the ground without any covering and we were all without clothing. We were fed a small portion of bread and water. Japanese machine guns were set up on all sides, ready to fire."

Soon afterward, it got worse.

Continued on page 117

DAVID M. GARINGER
Corporal
US MARINE CORPS

World War II

DAVID M. GARINGER
Spokane, Washington

Born in Omaha, Nebraska, David Garinger grew up in Colorado Springs and joined the Marines at age 19, following a brother who'd signed up four years earlier. David completed basic training in San Diego and soon began working in the motor transport company.

But he also discovered an additional skill. "We trained at a rifle range called Linda Vista," he recalls. "On the shooting range, I made sharp shooter with the M-1, and I got perfect with the 45 pistol."

From boot camp he traveled overseas in 1944 on the SS *President Taylor*. On the South Pacific island of Pavuvu, Garinger and 19 others were selected to transfer to the supply depot on Banika Island. "There was a lot going on over there," he says, "but I didn't see any action. We were too far south—and about 60 miles east of Guadalcanal."

Looking back now, David knows his life could have been cut short. "Three times, when I was in the Marines, I almost wound up going to Okinawa. I'm glad I didn't go, for I may not be here now."

Instead, he settled into life on Banika, working with fellow Marines as well as Navy and Army personnel. "My best friend was a corpsman in the Navy," he says.

Garinger performed a variety of duties. "I drove a bus and did carpentry. I was the designated company carpenter. I worked on buildings we needed in the motor transport company."

The small island contained an airstrip, large enough to accommodate DC-3 planes. But David found another purpose for it. "I used the airstrip myself. Nearly every night I would get out on the strip and run, which, I believe, is why I am as healthy as I am now."

Sometimes David found opportunities for sightseeing. He recalls an invitation to visit a neighboring island. "I couldn't go alone unless I was accompanied by the chaplain who held services for the natives, many of whom were Christians." So, on the chaplain's next excursion, David went along. He met several locals, with whom he struck a variety of bargains. "We traded stuff," he remembers. "One fella showed me a little room in his plywood hut where he had shelves full of canned Spam that he'd traded to our cooks for fruit."

When Garinger's enlistment was up, he left the Marines for a higher education. "Once I was out, I wondered if I should have stayed in, but I wanted to go to school," he says. "I finished my last year of high school and married Zelma who I met in high school. Then I went to college on the GI Bill. I graduated in 1951 from Seattle Pacific College, which now is a university."

Hoping to become a pastor, David studied Biblical literature and earned his BA in Old and New Testament. He and his wife had four children but discovered two problems with pastoring. "Being a pastor was not suited for me and the needs of my family, because the churches were small and the pay was not enough to cover our expenses," he says. He had to work as a carpenter to supplement his income.

Continued on page 119

BERNARD "NORM" KIEFFER
Corporal, Military Police
US ARMY

April 1929 ~ November 2008

World War II

BERNARD "NORM" KIEFFER
Spokane, Washington

Bernard A. "Norm" Kieffer grew up in New Philadelphia, Ohio, in 1929. While living in Michigan City, Indiana, Norm followed his older brother and sister into the service. He was anxious to serve his country and enlisted in the Army in November 1945, while only sixteen years of age.

He served as a corporal in the Army's 89th Military Police Company during the last days of World War II. Stationed in the Philippines at Manila from July 1946 to February 1947, he was a jeep driver and never saw combat.

Mary, his wife of 58 years, says unpleasant conditions affected Norm. "The hot, muggy weather took a toll on him," she recalls, "forcing him to change his uniform two or three times a day." Often the water was polluted, and the food preparation was very strange to him. While stationed there he caught malaria and suffered the affects of the disease for years to follow. He sustained an injury to his back during the service as a result of a jeep accident and was laid up for over a year and a half. He often mentioned traveling home via the Navy hospital ship USS *Hope*.

In spite of these difficulties, Norm returned to the states with positive memories of his army experience. He admired a superior officer named Terry and later named his first-born son after him.

After the war, Norm received a WWII Victory Medal, one Lapel Button and two Discharge Emblems. He was honorably discharged from the Army in 1947. Three years later he married Mary Di Ielsi and lived in Spokane, Washington, for 32 years. He had seven children, 24 grandchildren and 22 great-grandchildren with two more on the way

Unfortunately, Norm was unable to witness the completion of his portrait. He suffered a fall in November 2008 which resulted in a fatal head injury.

World War II Victory Medal

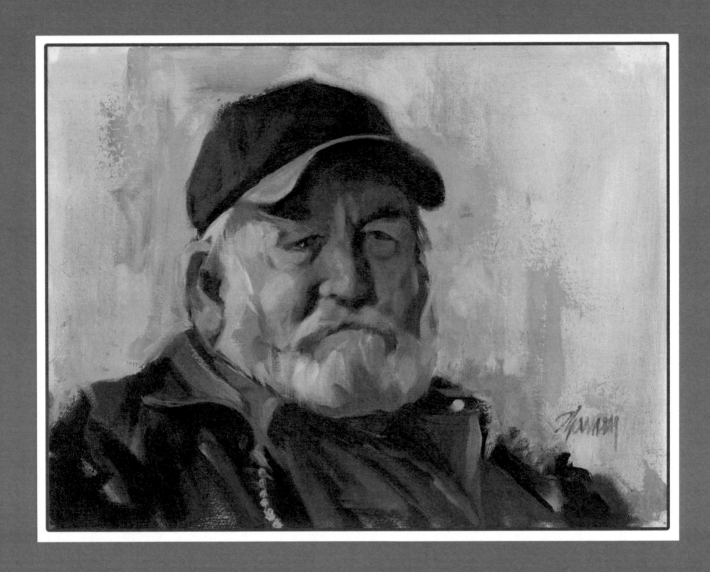

DAVID DEPUE
Seaman First Class
US NAVY

World War II ~ Korea

DAVID DEPUE
Old Town, Idaho

From his earliest years, David Depue understood self-sufficiency. Born in Kansas, he lived with his family on a farm, which they lost during the Great Depression. In desperation, they left by horse and wagon and arrived in Taney County, Missouri, two and a half months later. Settling into David's grandfather's home, the family made a life for themselves.

"My dad started operating my grandfather's grist mill, grinding grain and making flour and stuff like that, from oats and corn," David recalls. They worked hard and earned meager incomes. But the same could be said for their neighbors. "Nobody had any money then."

Still, they survived better than many others. David's grandfather raised cows, so the children drank milk. In addition, David says, "We had lots of wild hogs, so we had great pork to eat. Yeah, these were big pigs!"

The multi-generational family lived on the White River, which served as the state line between Arkansas and Missouri. When possible, they bartered for luxuries like coffee and sugar.

Many of David's relatives served in the military, including uncles and cousins in the Navy, and David's own father in the Army. When David turned 13, he joined the Missouri Armed Guard—a predecessor to the National Guard. He served two years, until the unit was activated for war. Before he could be shipped out, he says, "My mother went down and told them how old I was, so they kicked me out. I was 15."

When David turned 16, in 1945, His mother signed for him and he enlisted in the Navy, and he enjoyed it from the start. "Of course I was a big boy, so basic training was easy for me. I had worked [on the farm] since I was six years old, so I was pretty well developed. And, I had an attitude far superior to a kid because I knew how to work and help feed my family." He saw the physical training as a welcome challenge. "I loved the competition and the outdoing of everybody else."

Coming out of boot camp, he was promoted to Seaman Second Class, and he boarded the USS *Topeka*. A year later he made First Class. He worked on the *Topeka's* deck as a Boson's Mate, later known as Gunner's Mate. One of his duties was to train the "90-day wonders"—newly commissioned officers who needed practical experience. David enjoyed overseeing his superiors as they swabbed decks, tied knots, sewed leather and canvas, and covered lifelines.

David's career in the Navy took him across the Pacific. After a tour in Japan, he sailed to the Philippines. He remembers one "funny situation" while in Subic Bay, in 1947. "We'd been there a couple of days, aboard the cruiser *Atlanta*. After a few hours of liberty, I got back to the ship and realized I'd left my glasses in a dance hall."

He asked the Officer of the Deck for permission to use a military vehicle to go back and retrieve his glasses.

Continued on page 119

~ 17 ~

H. DEAN FURNESS
2nd Class / Athletic Specialist
US NAVAL AIR

World War II

H. DEAN FURNESS
Spokane, Washington

H Dean Furness joined the Navy Air on June 30, 1942, along with two buddies from high school. The three of them took a physical and were sworn in at night. Skipping basic training, they spent the following months building a Navy base in Pasco, Washington.

Soon, though, Furness received instruction as an aviation mechanic. Working in the "paint and dope shop," he stenciled numbers and letters on the planes. But by 1944 he found himself in combat.

"I went overseas to Japan for the Battle of Leyte,[1] on the USS Annie Arundel," he says. "Going in, we waded up to our ankles, then clear up to our knees. Then the fire started hitting." Although the Arundel had no weapons, several nearby jeep carriers sped to the scene. "They bombed the hell out of the beach," Dean recalls. "We were right there during the time the bombing was going on."

When the fighting subsided, Furness and his fellow sailors settled into tents during several months of relative peace. They even had time for recreation, including trading and bartering with locals. He recalls one incident in particular. "I made a deal for a monkey with a carton of cigarettes and a mattress cover." Dean and his nine-month-old friend stayed close. "It was the cutest little thing you ever saw. He was pretty small, and we had a lot of fun with him." Eventually he sold the monkey for $60.

Upon discharge, Furness traveled back to the United States. He returned to his previous job as a millwright for Centennial Mills. The company graciously took him back two days after he arrived and gave him two salary advancements.

"I have no gripes against the military," he asserts, looking back on his service and his re-entry into civilian life. "I was always treated right."

---

1 The Battle of Leyte Gulf was a World War II engagement between October 23 and October 26, 1944. It was the largest air-sea battle in history. American and Allied forces, preparing for the recapture of the Philippine island of Leyte, were met by the amassed forces of Imperial Japan. Despite significant losses, Allied ships and aircraft destroyed most of the Japanese fleet and ended its power as an effective fighting force. Having defended the landing force against the air and naval challenge, the Allied military opened the way for the re-conquest of Leyte by the land forces under the command of General Douglas MacArthur.

JOHN RUSSELL
Private First Class
US ARMY

World War II

JOHN RUSSELL
Moses Lake, Washington

As a resident of a facility for persons with developmental disabilities, John Russell had no idea he would eventually become a military medic in Korea.

From age two to 14, Russell lived at this eastern Washington facility. He had daily responsibilities, including chores like raising and lowering the flag. While at one of his duties, he met a girl who also lived there.

"I kissed this girl," John recalls, "and that was the first and only time I did it. Nothing happened, but they put the girl in a straight jacket, and put her in cold water to get her to say that we had sex, which we didn't."

Meanwhile, John says, his attendants moved him to an area "where they put old, disabled people and crazy people." Looking back, he believes residents in that wing were mistreated. "If I'd been left in there, I would never have lived to see the day."

So he decided to escape.

"I ran, and I must have had the Good Lord helping me, because I escaped through swamps with these dogs barking, and they were trying to find me but they couldn't." After an exhausting trek through the darkness, Russell unwittingly made his way to the home of an employee of the very facility he'd left. To his surprise, though, the family sympathized with him and loaded him into their car. "They took me to Spokane," he remembers. "On the way, the state patrol stopped us and said that there was a runaway and that he's very dangerous."

Russell, meanwhile, had stretched out on the back seat and had fallen asleep. The patrolman must not have noticed him there, because the family continued on their way. "They took me to a boarding house in Spokane where 30 girls who attended Kinman Business College boarded."

He lived there—in the basement by himself. Taking vocational classes at Lewis and Clark High School helped him hone his skills and improve his reading level. He spent free time setting pins at a nearby bowling alley.

In 1944 he enlisted and was soon shipped from San Francisco to the Pacific theater. For unknown reasons, his unit did not immediately go to Japan as planned. Instead, they stayed in the Pacific for 37 days. "That was about the time the A-bombs went off," he recalls, admitting that he and his buddies didn't know about the bombs until later. When his ship finally arrived in Japan, it didn't stay. "I was there just long enough to take pictures of the bomb and the dead in both Hiroshima and Nagasaki."

Korea was his destination, and there Russell became a medic. The job proved to be both difficult and memorable. "At the 'H' Station, I worked at night. I was responsible for people that had gonorrhea and syphilis. My job was to give them penicillin and their medications." If John determined a person's situation was extreme, he would transfer him to another hospital. This process occasionally resulted in hard feelings.

Continued on page 121

ERNEST FRAIJO
CO - 3rd Class
US NAVY

World War II ~ Korea

ERNEST FRAIJO
Spokane, Washington

Snow, snow, snow.

That's what Ernest Fraijo remembers most about boot camp at Farragut in January 1943. After all, growing up in East Los Angeles, he'd never seen snow. But he didn't mind. The thought of staying in L.A., with its gangs, didn't appeal to young Fraijo, age 17. Looking back, he says, "All I knew was street smarts. Street smarts, though, don't work in the military, because altogether it's a different language, a different way of living, and you are under a very strict disciplinary factor."

But he adapted well. After basic training, he served aboard the ARS 34 USS *Gear* for two and a half years. "It was primarily a salvage vessel," he says, "but we did see some action."

That action would come later; meanwhile, Fraijo worked in the kitchen as cook, baker and butcher.

The *Gear* and her sister ship, the USS *Clamp*,—a USS *Prairie* Command SOPA—worked in tandem around Guam, all under the command of Admiral Hoover. Fraijo remembers Admiral Hoover's nicknames for the two vessels. "The sister ship was The Ship of Thieves, and our ship was The Ship of Lunatics."

Perhaps Admiral Hoover had good reason for his choice of the term "lunatic." Fraijo recalls a particular shipmate. "We had one young man there whose dad was a state representative in Florida. He hung himself over the side of the ship, while we were underway, and cut his hair. He had his feet tied so he just hung there while the ship was going, cutting his hair. When we found him, he was about half drowned."

On another occasion, the *Gear* salvaged a sunken supply ship. "It had a lot of medicinal bottles of brandy," he describes. "The crew had a private diver bringing up the brandy, which we put underneath our bedding. The other ship, The Ship of Thieves, was tied with us. They were doing the same thing on the starboard side that our divers were going on the port side." As a result, both crews accumulated an impressive stock. "My locker was jammed with bottles of brandy," Fraijo says. "Though it was for medicinal purposes, I was selling mine."

But Fraijo didn't spend all his time selling brandy and baking bread. He remembers a dangerous combat situation near Iwo Jima, when he had to handle weapons. "My first job was as a spotter on a Quad 40. After that they needed somebody on the machine gun on the port side. They asked me if I would go, so I became a gunner on a twin 50-caliber air-cooled machine gun." He says it was hard to cock, and he had to be harnessed into a type of saddle while operating it.

One of his shipmates, a man named Ramiro, stood on the starboard side of the twin weapon, and Fraijo worked the port side. "We caught this Zero coming in," Fraijo says. "Everybody was shooting at him, and Ramiro was hitting him. When he came over to my side of the ship, well, I shot too; but I never hit him, I don't think." Moments later, though, they saw the plane nosedive into the water half a mile away.

Continued on page 121

WILLARD C. NEIGHBOUR
Corporal
US MARINE CORPS - 5th DIVISION

World War II

WILLARD C. NEIGHBOUR
Nine Mile Falls, Washington

In 1942 Willard Neighbour and a group of friends in Independence, Missouri, held an informal meeting. "We talked it over and decided the Marines was the place we wanted to go," Neighbour says. But in the next breath he admits, "Well, I've got second thoughts about that now."

He served as a radio/telephone technician on Iwo Jima. "Over there, you don't climb poles," he remembers. "It's all black-lava sand about 18 inches deep, and you take a step and you slide back half way." The island's highest point—only 500 feet above sea level—was the famous mountain memorialized in the photo of the U.S. flag-raising.

More unusual, Neighbour says, was the "underground city." He describes an intricate network of tunnels and caves. "You can walk underneath the island. Some caves were 30 feet high and 40 to 50 feet long."

When he and fellow soldiers arrived, they spent the first three days wading to and from shore, unloading Howitzer shells. Neighbour says, "There were three of them in a crate, and it was all a guy could do to lift them—they weighed well over 100 pounds—and haul them 400-500 yards." By the time they'd completed the job, he recalls, "our feet were just like prunes from three days in a row in salt water."

Neighbour and the others faced frequent danger on Iwo Jima, but sometimes one of them would disregard the seriousness of the situation. For example, he remembers a friend, nicknamed Scooch, operating radio and telephone from a foxhole. "A couple of Marines had just been shot," Neighbour says. But Scooch paid no attention, sitting with head and shoulders above ground.

Neighbour, believing snipers hid nearby, warned him. "Scooch, you're taking an awful chance. Why don't you get down deeper in the foxhole so you're not exposed?" For unknown reasons, the radioman ignored him, and about a half-hour later he was shot in the head, dying instantly.

But not all incidents had such tragic endings. Neighbour remembers another situation with a different result. After hearing a series of shots from the enemy, a soldier yelled, "They got me! They got me!" But actually, his canteen—strapped to his hip—had taken the hit. Neighbour says, "The water was running down his rear, and he thought it was blood."

In spite such lighthearted moments, most of Neighbour's memories on Iwo Jima involve loss of life. He recalls one short period of time—30 to 45 minutes—when his company fired on approximately 1500 of the enemy below them. As the battle concluded, he says, "there were just a few of them left."

Likewise, the tunnels and caves became enemy tombs. Neighbour and his friend Mitchell would approach a cave and shout to the Japanese soldiers—in their own language—to surrender. "Most wouldn't," Neighbour says. "So when they refused to come out, we went right up to the mouth of the cave with a big charge of TNT. Everything that was in there was blown up."

Continued on page 123

WILLIAM GOLDFOOS
Tech Sergeant
US ARMY AIR FORCE

World War II

WILLIAM GOLDFOOS
Manson, Washington

William Goldfoos explains his involvement in military aviation in the 1940s: "We had no idea what an important part of history we were playing."

Enlisting at 17 ("Yeah, I kind of lied about my age"), he joined the Air Force because he wanted to fly. His father, an amputee from WWI, encouraged him, and he entered basic training with gusto. Unfortunately, he developed a physical problem during this time, and "medically washed out of the flying program." Still, he found a way to work with planes. "I went into another program that was available for me—jet aircraft—an area that was new to the military."

His first assignment took him to Chanute AFB in Illinois. There, he helped develop the prototype P80 by adapting Allison J33 and J35 engines, which had been built in England. "We had our own hangar," Goldfoos recalls. "It was guarded and off-limits to everybody. We had special badges to get in."

Next, he was transferred to Walker AFB in Roswell, New Mexico. "This was the 509th Bomb Wing," he explains. "These people were the ones that flew the *Enola Gay* and dropped the atomic bomb, the Area 51 crowd." Goldfoos joined the 393rd Bomb Squadron, and his first job was maintenance on the *Enola Gay*, even though it wasn't a jet aircraft.

"The *Enola Gay* was the plane that took Fat Boy to Hiroshima and then to Nagasaki. Colonel Tibbitts was the pilot." William recalls seeing Tibbitts every day for months. "He was the last crewmember really to be with the airplane."

But Tibbitts never revealed his opinions about dropping the bombs. In fact, William said no one knew what the man was thinking. The aloof Colonel Tibbitts didn't socialize with Corporal Goldfoos, and their conversations dealt only with the mechanics of the plane. Nonetheless, Goldfoos remembers one tender detail about their relationship: "He called me Goldie."

In the years since his service, William has never determined why he was assigned the *Enola Gay*. His best guess? "We were just maintaining the plane because they had no idea what to do with it," he says. "They kept it on the ground, and there was always some notion about what to do, like send it to the bone yard because there were many threats made to Colonel Tibbitts."

After months on the *Enola Gay*, William and his crew shifted to B29s and B50s—just as the Korean Conflict broke out. He greatly preferred the new assignment. "I had this thrill about jet aircraft," he confesses. He was even more thrilled when transferred to the Second Strategic Support Squadron. There, he trained to become a loadmaster, the person who determines weight and balance for large transport aircraft.

Citing safety concerns, the military moved the squadron from Walker AFB to Castle AFB near Merced, California. About that time, the C124, with its four engines and clam-shelled door, was introduced. Goldfoos

Continued on page 124

OTIS STUTES
SFC E-7
US ARMY

1922 ~ 2008

World War II

OTIS STUTES
Spokane, Washington

At age 18, Otis Stutes believed "the spirit of the nation" compelled him to enlist, so he left the family farm in Pleasanton, Kansas, in 1940.

The next few decades he gave to the military, on the beaches of Normandy and in the jungles of Vietnam, in frigid Greenland and humid Korea. He saw numerous battles and survived three wars, and he received a variety of awards, including the Purple Heart, the Bronze Star and a Presidential Citation.

As his son, Tom, says, "He was a good soldier."

Among the first Americans to be deployed to France after the Battle of Normandy, Stutes and his buddies learned more than warfare; they learned survival. For example, when fishing near the beach to supplement their meager rations, they used percussion grenades. Stutes pulled the pin, threw the grenade into the water and took cover. After the boom, countless fish floated to the surface. The men feasted that night. In another instance—this time in Germany—Stutes went deer hunting. He didn't spot a deer, but he and others located a herd of cattle. Thanks to the meat cutters in their division, everyone enjoyed steaks along with c-rations.

Of course, survival involved much more than a square meal. It also meant dodging bullets and squeaking by in close calls. During the Battle of the Bulge, Stutes and his unit were not chosen for a reconnaissance mission. As a result, they avoided the nearby Malmedy Massacre of December 17, 1944, in which scores of soldiers were killed by their German captors.

A short time later, Stutes and two officers rode atop a half-track, a tank-like vehicle with regular wheels on the front and caterpillar tracks on the rear. Stutes realized the Germans could see their position, and he warned his officers. But it was too late. An enemy shell struck, sending shrapnel into the gas tanks and killing the two officers instantly. Stutes himself took shrapnel in the legs. Miraculously, his helmet received a direct hit, leaving a one-inch hole, but his head wasn't even scratched.

On a third close call, Stutes and a friend stood talking. From nowhere a sniper's shot rang out, and the friend was hit between the eyes. "It was the weirdest thing," Stutes once said, "because we were just talking, and all of a sudden this guy was gone." The man was married with two daughters, and Stutes wasn't married at the time. He often wondered why he survived and the family man did not.

Other near-misses included one in which Stutes himself was holding the weapon. He'd captured four enemy soldiers and was walking them back to the camp. When he heard laughter from a couple of them, he made threatening gestures. Lifting his gun, he pointed toward the four, indicating his intention to restore order. The gun accidentally discharged, and the shot barely missed the prisoners. As Stutes' son tells it, "He split 'em with just a burst of fire, and they instantly shut up."

Continued on page 122

Korea

JOHN KOZOL
Staff Sergeant
US ARMY CORPS of ENGINEERS

February 1933 ~ September 2009

Korea

JOHN KOZOL
Spokane, Washington

Professional baseball or a stint in the Army?

John Kozol had an offer for each—at the same time. After graduating from high school in Bethlehem, Pennsylvania, he got a call from the Arizona Cardinals, which was the triple-A team for St. Louis. But he also got a draft notice from Uncle Sam. He says, "I could have played major-league baseball, but then that crazy war came along and changed my life."

He's referring to the Korean conflict, during which he served in the Army Corp of Engineers, First Calvary Division. He worked in Seoul and later transferred to Hokkaido, Japan.

"I was the driver and radio man for a general, who had a lot of secrets," he recalls. "It was an honor to drive the general around and do his radio work." But he believes the officer lacked moral character. Kozol transported him to town twice a week, and "he'd get so shaken that I got to hang around for a couple days when he gets done whatever he's doing, pick him up, and take him back to the base. I was like a bodyguard."

Nevertheless, Kozol respected the general in his military life. "He was very much a by-the-book guy. He'd get orders and follow them right down to the T. No diversification. Yeah, he was a good guy. I can't complain about the way he treated me, but I'm just saying that some of the things he did . . . The wife and three kids at home . . . well, that's the way it goes."

As the general's aide, Kozol had occasional opportunities for life-and-death actions. He recalls one such incident. The general, located a few miles north, was expecting Kozol to pick him up the next day. But, Kozol says, "I was in bed when on the radio we had an attack coming in from the North. Something told me to get out of bed and go pick him up a day early." He drove up to the general's camp and woke him out of a sound sleep. "I said 'Don't ask me why, General, but we got to get the hell out of here.' He listened to me; we got out of there. Next thing you know, it's totaled."

Kozol smiles as he recalls, "Oh, yeah, he was a very grateful man."

Spending almost five and a half years in the military, Kozol worked as a CCIW operator for the general. The position required a high level of security clearance, and at one point the chain of command discovered that Kozol's grandfather was Russian. "Somebody decided I was a Communist. Man, they went through paperwork like you wouldn't believe!" He says his orders were frozen for about six months—until the situation was rectified and he received his clearance.

Looking back, Kozol says his military days prepared him for the years that followed. "I picked up some good training and experience in the service that carried over into civilian life." He learned public relations during his time under the general. "I had to be good with people. So when I came out I wound up in sales and never had trouble getting good work. For instance, I was one of the general managers in Black Angus

Continued on page 125

BOBIE EBY
E-6 First Class
US ARMY

Korea

BOBIE EBY
Bonners Ferry, Idaho

In 1932, a horse-drawn wagon brought a doctor to the doorstep of a tiny dwelling in rural South Dakota, where he delivered Bobie Eby on a snowy December night. Eby now calls his humble home a "toilet-paper shack," which had no running water or electricity. Within a couple of years the family moved to Bonners Ferry, Idaho, and there he grew up.

Three older brothers fought in World War II, and Bobie signed on after they all came home safely. Inducted in 1950, Bobie finished boot camp at Fort Ord. He says his early Army experience "wasn't too bad, because I was a company boxer." While still in high school, he'd trained hard and boxed competitively, so he relished the challenge in boot camp. "I'd go to the gym and work out with trainers to get ready for the smoker every Friday night," he says. "I'd fight kids from New York, all over. It didn't make a difference where they were from, because I was in good shape. I was a light-weight, 135 pounds."

After basic training, Eby chose leadership school, but it was interrupted because of the Korean conflict. He soon found himself bound for Southeast Asia. "They flew us from Seattle to Alaska to and then to Tokyo to join the outfit to go to Korea," he remembers. "They flew us to Tokyo in one of them old four-motor drop planes that had nothing but stretchers in them to bring back the wounded and sick."

He joined the Seventh Division, 31st Field Artillery, and eventually landed at Inchon. "We went in just like boot camp, you know, with the weapons marching. We got up to the Seoul River and dug a hole about two feet deep in the sand. I was taking a nap, the last of August—a nice, sunny day for a nap. And then," he says, "all hell broke loose."

Eby and his buddies faced a sudden volley of machine-gun fire, mortars and other rounds. But thanks to the foxholes they'd dug, they managed to survive. However, they later realized survival would become even more challenging in the days ahead. During the following winter, they endured temperatures of 40 below zero. They also faced Chinese soldiers who wanted retaliation for the 100-pound rounds they were receiving from the Americans.

Eby served in a forward outfit, surveying the layout of the land to prepare for his unit's next movement. "I started out as the number-five man, and then I went from five to number one, so I'm shooting a 155." Even though he realizes the danger he faced and the enemy he destroyed, he speaks without emotion about the seriousness of his duties. "I got to pull the trigger. It was just a job."

When Eby completed his enlistment, he joined the Idaho National Guard and "went back to the woods sawing logs." After a particularly snowy winter in Idaho, he moved to Delano, California, and worked in his brother-in-law's auto-body business. But the hot summers forced him to reconsider, and five years later he returned to the Northwest. Through it all, he spent almost three decades in the Reserves and the National Guard.

Continued on page 125

LLOYD HUMPHREY
First Sergeant
US ARMY

Korea

LLOYD HUMPHREY
Kettle Falls, Washington

Lloyd Humphrey wanted to follow in the footsteps of his great-great uncle, purportedly the youngest soldier in the Union Army during the Civil War.

So he tried to enlist at age 13.

His plan almost worked: an uncle, who'd been a sailor, was to meet Lloyd at the recruiting office and sign for him. The only favor the uncle requested in return was money for a pint of wine. But Lloyd made the mistake of paying the man before they went to the recruiting office. The uncle got drunk and didn't show up.

Two years later, Lloyd tried again. A big boy for age 15, he stood nearly six feet tall and weighted 165 pounds. This time, another uncle vouched for him, and Lloyd joined the military—without the consent or knowledge of his parents.

Like his gymnast father, the younger Humphrey could accomplish amazing physical feats. Because of that, his training sergeant didn't like him. Humphrey believes the sergeant resented his abilities and punished him accordingly. If, for example, he did one-armed pull-ups or push-ups, the sergeant would demand that he do more. If Humphrey did Russian pushups—from a hand-stand against the wall—the sarge would require more, even though no one else in the platoon could do any at all.

Humphrey says the sergeant seemed intent on getting him into trouble. On one occasion, the sarge promised him a pass to a Bob Hope show, on the condition that Humphrey finish some extra duties. Humphrey did finish, and when he went back to the barracks, he caught the sergeant at his bunk. "There he was," he recalls, "clipping every fourth button off my class-A khaki uniforms with his little knife."

So Humphrey knew with certainty that the sergeant hated him.

In another instance, Sarge assigned Humphrey to late-night guard duty, watching over a pile of training grenades and other ammunition. After a few hours, Humphrey heard a jeep approach, but it stopped before reaching him. Hoping the driver might be bringing chow, he waited and watched. But no chow appeared. Instead, he saw shadows in the darkness, and one of them seemed to move.

Like other soldiers at the time, Humphrey had been warned about the possibility of a Russian invasion near Fort Ord. In his imagination he saw dozens of moving shadows. What if they were all Russians? He decided to devise makeshift ammunition from a box of blanks among the training supplies. Fairly certain a blank would do nothing more than spurt a flame at the end of the barrel, he added a booster into the barrel. And to keep the booster from falling out, he grabbed leaves from a shrub and tamped them down with a branch.

Continued on page 125

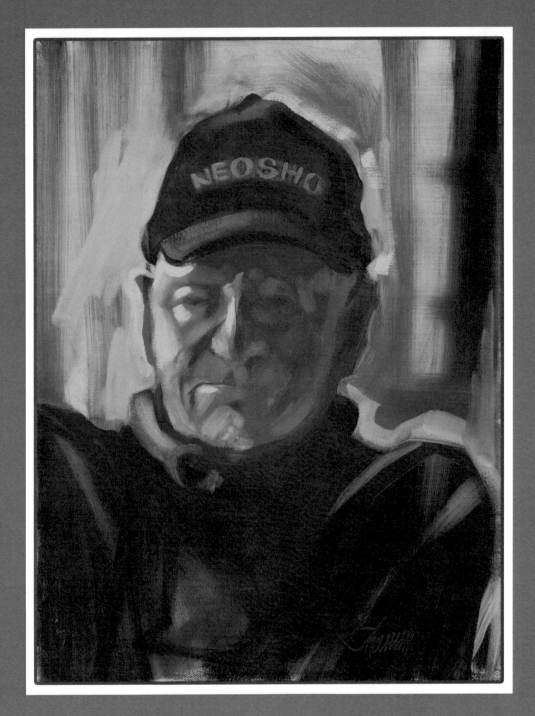

MARTIN PEGNAM
Corpsman
US NAVY

1934 ~ 2005

Korea

MARTIN PEGNAM
Bisbee, Arizona

Basic training at Bainbridge, Maryland, in July 1953 did not prepare Martin Pegnam adequately—at least not for an uncomfortable social situation involving a high-ranking official.

The event took place in the home of Martin's uncle, Cardinal Spellman[1] of New York. Days earlier, when the Cardinal had invited Martin, the young recruit didn't realize the luncheon would include a distinguished guest. His uncle had simply said, "Come visit, because there's somebody you should meet, and we'll have lunch."

Martin arrived—in uniform, of course—and the housekeeper showed him to the living room. There sat the admiral, with the host nowhere in sight. Martin stood in mortification, wondering how to make small talk to an admiral. Fortunately, his uncle soon came into the room, laughing, and rescued him.

Even without training in social skills, Pegnam did well in other areas. From Bainbridge, he was sent to the Philadelphia Naval Hospital, where he became a corpsman and achieved the rank of HM-2. Next he transferred to a hospital in Naples, Italy.

According to his wife, Nancy, one of the most memorable aspects of Martin's life involved his love of reading and storytelling. "In boot camp," she says, "he got several buddies to start reading. Guys who had never read began reading because of his influence." Whenever he had time off, Martin read and gladly shared his books with those around him. His friends fondly referred to his book collection as the Martin Pegnam Naval Library.

During part of his four-year enlistment, he was stationed on the oiler *Neosho*, first in the Mediterranean and later dry-docked in Virginia. Throughout his time on board, Pegnam worked as a teacher of therapeutic exercise. He enjoyed his time on the *Neosho*, and years later he and his wife visited Neosho, Indiana, while traveling. Nancy recalls, "He got a sweatshirt and a cap there." She says the ship was named after the Neosho River, and the town proudly touted its connection to the naval vessel with souvenirs and historical displays.

---

1 Born in Whitman, Massachusetts, in 1889, Francis Joseph Spellman attended Fordham University and the American College at Rome while preparing to enter the priesthood. He received his ordination as a Roman Catholic priest in 1916 and in 1924 was named archivist of the Archdiocese of Boston. Later the following year, Spellman went on pilgrimage to Rome and was subsequently appointed the first American assistant to the papal secretariat of state. Remaining in Rome between 1925 and 1931, Spellman was forced to leave the Vatican when the church hierarchy assigned him the dangerous mission of smuggling an antifascist encyclical out of Italy.
In 1932, Spellman returned to the United States and was quickly appointed auxiliary bishop of Boston, a position he retained until 1939 when Pope Pius XII made him archbishop of New York and vicar of the United States Armed Forces (a position that charged him with overseeing spiritual services to all Roman Catholics in the U.S. military). Skillfully using his newfound prestige in the American Catholic hierarchy, Spellman was instrumental in mobilizing American Catholics behind the war effort. For his efforts he was again rewarded by Pius XII in 1946 when the Pope elevated him to the College of Cardinals.

Continued on page 126

PHILLIP A. BREN
Captain
US AIR FORCE

Korea ~ Cold War

PHILLLIP A. BREN
Dunsmuir, California

Growing up in Grandview, Washington, Phil Bren enjoyed a stable childhood. "Plenty to eat, lots of good healthy work, no booze for me, absolutely no drugs," he says, looking back. "This was a comforting, progressive environment."

He and his friends spent their summers in the fields, picking apples, cherries and pears, and cutting asparagus. They also worked shaking potato vines in front of the picker, who then grabbed potatoes from the ground. "I got a penny for each full sack, and made about five dollars a day—pretty good money back then!"

He joined the military after townspeople "badgered" him. "They wanted to draft me into the Navy and send me off to Korea, but I quickly joined the Air Force, on 18 June 1954." Fresh out of high school, Phil finished basic training at Lackland and chose the medical field for his career.

"From 1954 to 1958 I worked at Sheppard AFB in Texas and Luke AFB in Arizona," he says. While at Luke, he and his unit provided support for local airports. They helped with occasional incidents, but a particularly traumatic event is seared into his memory. "One time we gathered up all the body bags we could find because two commercial jets ran into each other and crashed into the Grand Canyon. We had to go back in there and pick up parts of people laying all over the landscape for miles."

After completing his enlistment, Phil stayed in the Air Force Reserve while attending Washington State University. He was promoted to staff sergeant, then graduated as second lieutenant in 1962. He went on to officer training school and earned a commission.

One of his first duties as an officer involved the measuring of the North American continent. "We used a satellite for triangulations between stars to determine the exact positions of any place on earth. My work was to analyze these pictures of the stars and prepare them for the mathematicians."

In 1966 Lt. Bren was reassigned to Germany for three years as a nuclear weapons officer. He explains his function: "The English had two engine bombers that were stationed around Germany, ready to fly in quick-reaction areas. They would fly 100 feet off the ground, and we provided nuclear weapons for them. They flew below radar level, so the Russians could never stop them."

But Bren noticed the British pilots wore only a jump suit when they flew. "They had no parachute, nothing. I asked a British officer once, and he said, 'Well, you know, I don't think we'll be coming back.'"

In spite of the danger, Bren sees excitement in his military career. "I was at Check Point Charlie when the Soviets occupied East Berlin," he recalls. "I remember one time I was at the Brandenburg Gate on the East German side. I knew there were German shepherds in a slot between the two fences. There was a warning sign on the Soviet side that said 67 people died trying to escape. I asked the German guard, 'I understand you have dogs between these walls?' He denied it. So I gave a big whistle, and these dogs came out and started jumping

Continued on page 127

Cold War

TOM McLAUGHLIN
Private 1st Class
US ARMY

Date of Service 1954 ~ 1957
Cold War

TOM MCLAUGHLIN
Deer Park, Washington

Wouldn't you know it?

Tom McLaughlin's high school friend led a handful of his buddies to enlist in the military in 1954. They all followed this ringleader, some joining the Naval Air Reserve and some joining the Army. The only problem was that Tom's friend couldn't pass the physical. He remained a civilian while his friends donned uniforms.

McLaughlin chose the Army and went to Fort Ord, California, for Basic. "I didn't mind the training," he says as he looks back. "I was in a lot better shape than most. We had a lot of draftees that were overweight, college-educated and out of shape but were still enlisted men. The six-mile march and all that never bothered me because I was 17 years old. Plus I was in good shape."

But he had one problem with boot camp: "I just didn't like people telling me what to do." He says his undisciplined home life hadn't prepared him for military structure. As a teen, he had no curfew and sometimes stayed away from home for days. So, when the Army required him "to be in bed every night at a certain time and get up at a certain time," he says, he balked. The nine-week Basic took him almost nine months, "because of my frequent vacations—that is, unauthorized vacations."

Finally he managed to finish and got orders for Fairbanks, Alaska. There he joined an engineer battalion, thanks to his experience with heavy equipment while working for his father. His duties at Fairbanks, he says, "varied from building roads, parade grounds, baseball diamonds, hockey rinks, artillery range, and just about anything moving the earth."

Also, every winter his battalion traveled with the infantry, carrying food and supplies. He remembers one cold night during an excursion. "We had 55-mph winds and 60 below zero. Tents blew down. We didn't lose anybody, but we weren't real warm."

McLaughlin's stint in the Army proved to be a turning point for him. "That was three years in my life where I learned some discipline," he says. "I hadn't had any before." In addition, he attributes his positive experience to the relatively stable international scene. "The morale was good when I was in the service. It was peacetime then. There wasn't any war going on. Korea was over with and Vietnam hadn't started."

After his discharge, McLaughlin used his skills to transition into civilian life. "The work I had been doing in the service pretty much carried over into what I've been doing for another 40 years," he states. "I had learned quite a bit, the practical experience of running equipment—plus blueprint reading." For him, the military "was like a really good trade school."

Today, though he's lost contact with most of his buddies from high school, Tom McLaughlin maintains many of the friendships he established in the Army. "My best friend was killed about ten years ago in a farm

Continued on page 127

RONALD DECKER
Private 1st Class
US ARMY NATIONAL GUARD

Date of Service 1957 ~ 1962
Cold War

RONALD DECKER
Chicago, Illinois

With a smile, Ronald Decker says, "My military career was totally undistinguished." He enlisted after a college degree and two years at law school in Chicago. Still, he remembers one outstanding aspect of the military: "The food was better than at college."

Decker enjoyed basic training—even at Fort Knox in winter. He liked learning about weapons, and he discovered various applications for them, both official and unofficial. For example, he says, "I learned that when they came around looking for someone to do dirty work, I would immediately take my rifle apart and start cleaning it. They would glance at me and say, 'Oh don't get him; he's busy cleaning his rifle.'"

But his military career had a serious side as well. After boot camp he went to Fort Dix for advanced infantry training and additional wilderness drills. He finished six months of training and then returned to Chicago to complete his law degree, where he transferred to an Illinois National Guard artillery battalion. The military allowed this come-and-go arrangement for only a brief period. As Decker explains, "I joined after Korea and before Vietnam. The Defense Department adopted a scheme whereby a draft-eligible man could serve six months of active duty followed by 5.5 years in the active reserves. As I recall, this was done because, after the end of the Korean War, the military did not need so many active-duty personnel."

While in the reserves, Decker attended weekly drills in Chicago at the old Chicago Avenue Armory. And each summer, he went to a two-week camp and honed his weapons skills. "We actually fired our 105mm howitzers," he says. "That was the only time we fired the howitzers." He was part of a six-man gun crew, and he hand-loaded the shells weighing about 30 pounds each.

Soon he graduated to a less physical role. "I would stand back behind the guns and make calculations on topographic maps to direct the guns to the targets and shout numbers to the men on the guns." Even though computers now perform this function, Decker says the late 1950s hadn't yet reached that point. "We still used the WWII technology of sticking pins in a topographic map and making measurements to fire the gun," he says. But he didn't mind. "I have had a life-long interest in maps, so it was enjoyable to have a job that used maps."

Of course, not all military skills transfer into civilian life. He notes, "Firing howitzers had no application whatsoever to my career as a corporate lawyer."

Because he enlisted during peacetime, Decker didn't see actual combat. But his first three-year enlistment was extended by one year because of the Berlin Crisis in the early 1960s. Even so, he was never deployed, and the military surprised him by releasing him from the final years of his obligation. He was discharged in 1962, following five years of service.

Undistinguished?

Continued on page 128

RON VIETZKE
Airman E-3
US Naval Air Reserve

Date of Service 1954 ~ 1962
Cold War

RON VIETZKE
Airway Heights, Washington

Victory gardens. War bonds. Rationing of sugar and gasoline.

Ron Vietzke remembers all those details of living through World War II, though he was only nine when the conflict ended. He also recalls watching German POWs build a hospital, and his mother's attempt to get an old tire fixed, because no new ones could be purchased.

Such memories helped shape the boy into the young man who, eight years later, enlisted with 14 friends from North Central High School in Spokane.

Unlike people entering today's basic training, those recruits attended an abbreviated, two-week boot camp. They spent a week marching and a week in survival classes. "It was a good thing to go through," he says. "We were just 17-year-old kids. When those two weeks were done, we were in the Navy."

Vietzke served in a variety of aircraft, including a P2V Neptune. He was also a part of a submarine squadron and a transport squadron. He remembers being injured in an unusual way. "I was carrying a bunch of parachutes, and someone had left the station hatch open in the back of the fuselage. I didn't see it, and I fell out of the airplane."

The damage would have been fatal, except for one thing: "Fortunately, we were on the ground," he says, so he didn't have far to fall. But he twisted his knee and was taken by ambulance to the hospital. When he came out, he says, "I was put on six weeks' active duty at Sandpoint. Light duty, because I had a cast on, so they put me standing guard at the Main Gate."

A potentially more dangerous event occurred later in Vietzke's military career. "I was in a Beach 18, which was a twin-engine, five-passenger plane." Flying at night, the men sat with their parachutes hanging from the backs of their seats. "All of a sudden," Vietzke says, "the engines start quitting and the pilots are up there yelling at each other, 'No! Turn that on. Wait! Try that!'" Vietzke and the four commanding officers sitting with him all reached for their parachutes. In the heat of the moment, he remembers, "one guy picked his up by the ripcord and opened it up—right inside the airplane!" The look on the officer's face gave a moment of comic relief in an otherwise tense situation.

But the passengers didn't have to use their chutes, because the pilots managed to execute an emergency landing in Sulfur Springs, Texas. Choosing that particular location turned out to be a wise decision, considering the plane had less than 15 minutes of fuel left. However, one issue further marred the situation. The landing gears on this airplane were wider than the taxiway.

Continued on page 128

DAVID M. NORDBY
E-5
US NAVAL AIR RESERVE

Date of Service 1954 ~ 1962
Cold War

DAVID NORDBY
St. George, Utah

David Nordby remembers living off the land in 1954.

One of a dozen or so high school friends from Spokane who joined the Naval Air Reserve together, he spent a week of boot camp in wilderness training. He and his buddies, enduring the same training as Air Force recruits, managed to get lost, jump off cliffs, eat snakes and wild mushrooms, and forage for roots—all in November in the Cusick area of northern Washington.

But that was the easy part.

"Then we went through the pressure chamber," Nordby says, "and I broke an eardrum in there. Blood came out of my nose and ears, and I've never had any hearing in the left ear since then."

Still, he kept going. He was assigned to NAS Geiger Field near Spokane. When it closed about three years later, he and many of his friends transferred to Seattle. "We were in a Cougar jet squadron, made up of ten 9F6's. These were aircrafts that were flown in Korea, and a lot of those pilots were old Korean War vets and WWII Navy carrier pilots," he remembers. He now wishes he'd talked to more of them and heard their stories.

But one person—though not a pilot—did make a lasting impression on Nordby. "I remember one of the guys was older, and when we would line up for inspection he was the only guy in the line that had a Purple Heart on his chest. He was wounded putting guys ashore in Italy." This man, an aviation electrician, unofficially watched out for the younger ones. "He taught school there, and he had a master's degree in physics," Nordby says, but the man never wanted to become a chief. "He said he'd rather mess around with us young guys. We were a lot more fun."

Nordby completed flight training at Sand Point Naval Air Station near Seattle, where he flew anti-sub patrols for four years. Eventually he became an aircrew instructor. Describing his typical duties, he says, "I was in this aircraft, with the two pilots up front, and two guys that ran the submarine detection in the back. I was in charge of radar and sonar, electronic countermeasures and magnetic air-borne detection gear."

Next, he was transferred to Los Alameda. At his first meeting after the move, his group was activated for the Berlin Crisis. "I was flying out of there as an aircrew guy, just a grunt," he says. "I flew the electronics and the radar out there in the ocean."

But what about his hearing loss? How could he deal with that in the military? "I always had problems with that one ear, but I wanted to keep flying," he explains. "The only way was to have the flight surgeon write me off as being a hundred percent good, and I let them do that."

Continued on page 128

ALLAN R. PRATT
Private First Class
US ARMY

Date of Service 1956 ~ 1958
Cold War

ALLAN R. PRATT
Hopkinton, Massachusetts

In November 1956, Al Pratt knew he was on the short list, so he signed up instead of waiting to be drafted. "I didn't enlist and I wasn't drafted, but I 'volunteered' for the draft," he says sarcastically.

Boot camp in early winter at Fort Lewis can be brutal. "It was dark and dreary, no snow, but very cold," he recalls. Nonetheless, the weather didn't get him down. "We were all in the same boat. We were all draftees or volunteer drafts, and so we emotionally supported one another. It went by really fast."

When he got his orders, he was shipped to New Jersey for electronics training. The move surprised him, he says, because he'd scored high on every aptitude test except electronics. Guessing the brass's motives, Pratt says, "They felt that because of my high scores in other categories, I would be a candidate for this particular course, which needed some students."

But he arrived at the training facility two weeks early. "So they put me on KP in the mess hall for those two weeks. My memory of that place is they were serving liver for dinner, and I had to pound on liver all morning. That was my job and I'll never forget that as long as I live."

Upon completing the electronics course, Pratt was transferred to New Mexico, "to a nuclear weapons school, a classified/civilian installation." There he attended training in Atomic Assembly Electrical (AAE), during the early stages of the Intercontinental Ballistic Missile (ICBM) program. Eventually he served in a nuclear weapons storage facility, where he delivered bombs to Air Force planes. He held this position for several months--until a problem arose.

"I got kicked out," he says.

The situation had begun when Pratt and his crew delivered a weapon known as a "bunker buster." Designed with a timed setting, this bomb would hit the ground and penetrate without detonating. At a later time it would be set to detonate. But in this particular case, Pratt recalls, "The pilot took off and was doing maneuvers when he discovered during these diving routines that the tail had fallen off of the bomb." An investigation followed, and Pratt's unit was blamed. As "low man on the totem pole," he says he took the fall and had to transfer out of the weapons depot.

He fulfilled the next several months of his military obligation in the library. "It was a huge building that had several fences around it and dogs. No windows," he recalls, stating that it was "a little claustrophobic in there." Within the library was a secure section, which was like a big safe. "All the classified books were in there, so I had to learn where all the books were. The professors, when they had classes, would come and check out the books. I made sure they had their books."

Continued on page 128

ROBERT LEE
E-4
US ARMY

Date of Service 1961 ~ 1967
Cold War

ROBERT LEE
Spokane, Washington

Even though he had two years of ROTC when he graduated from the University of Idaho, Robert Lee couldn't have imagined himself in the military. Instead, he followed his father's footsteps and got a job with an accounting firm in Portland. But a few months later, a piece of mail changed his plans.

"By September," he says, "I received the letter and was inducted on September 28, 1961."

After basic training, during which Lee scored high in combat proficiency, he transferred to Fort Leonard Wood on New Year's Day, 1962. He became an accounting specialist, but when the call came for helicopter pilots, he took and passed the test. However, he decided not to enroll in the training after all. "I would have six years added to my service obligation," he explains, "and I backed away from that." In hindsight, Lee believes the military needed pilots in anticipation of the Vietnam conflict.

He recalls another incident to support his theory. One day in the barracks, a guy who borrowed his jacket refused to return it. Lee says, "I caught him by the back of the neck, and he turned and hit me along the side of my head. I hit him once and down he went." He got his jacket back—along with a broken finger and bloody knuckles. The next morning he visited the doctor and the MPs, and soon he and the other guy were called into the company commander's office. Lee says he'll never forget one of the officer's comments: "Well, if you two boys want to fight, I know a place where I can send you. It's called Vietnam."

By the following spring, Lee got orders for Korea. "I was assigned to the 8th Army Finance and stayed there for 13 months," he recalls. As time passed, fellow accountants started shipping out, and Lee heard they were going to temporary duty in Thailand. Later, he found out the operation in Thailand was a funding operation for activities in Vietnam.

Lee had occasional opportunities to travel while in Korea. Once he took a tour of the Demilitarized Zone, and he made several visits to an orphanage, which his finance group supported. While there, he played with the children, including twin girls.

Because of his involvement in the financial aspect of the military, Lee understood the swapping of U.S. currency for Military Payment Certificates (MPCs). "Every GI in Korea turned in their US dollars as they arrived," he says. "The finance office collected the greenbacks, and we kept them stored in a big vault. Periodically there would be a flight to Japan and we would take the US dollars." He says the reason for this process was "to keep the U.S. dollars from entering the Korean economy." Also during his tour in Korea, the Military Payment Certificates in circulation were exchanged for a new issue of MPCs. He says the reason for this process was, "to make the older issue of MPCs worthless that had entered the Korean economy by U.S. soldiers' spending activities."

Continued on page 129

NORMAN WIEGELE
Spec 4 E-4
US ARMY

Date of Service 1961 ~ 1967
Cold War

NORMAN WIEGELE
Spokane, Washington

Norm Wiegele had one simple ambition in life: "All I wanted to do was be a truck driver." So he was happy in a transportation company's light-truck unit after boot camp. "When I ended up at Fort Ord, driving a deuce and a half out in the desert, well that's what I wanted," he says, describing the two-and-a-half ton truck he handled.

Later, he was shipped to Bremerhaven, Germany. Attached to the 89th Transportation Company, he assumed he'd continue driving trucks or heavy equipment. But the Army had a surprise for him, and Wiegele says, "I never ended up doing that at all."

Instead, he had an interview with an officer. "He asked me what kind of schooling I'd had," so Wiegele told him about two years of junior college and a semester at the University of Idaho. Next, the officer asked if he could type, offering a desk job if he was interested. "I jumped on the bandwagon right there, even though I wanted to be a heavy-equipment operator," Wiegele says, noting a variety of perks. "No KP, no guard duty, no nothing, five days per week. I had time to play baseball, basketball and football."

Wiegele worked as a personnel clerk specialist, processing people into the company or mustering them out. Even better, he says, he became a platoon leader soon after arriving in Germany. "I had my own squad, with many different nationalities. I had three African-Americans, a couple Hawaiians, a German—great kids. My two best friends were a Hawaiian and a German. I mean, I hung around with them probably more than anybody."

He and his friends—especially his buddy Clarence—found opportunities to travel. "We went to Italy a couple of times, to Rome." As a Catholic, he had a keen interest in one important tourist spot. "I went to the Vatican and was included in a picture with Pope Paul."

Wiegele remembers their unusual travel accommodations. "We were packed into the trains, and everybody sat on the floor. There was a lot of salami, a lot of bread, and a lot of wine. It was a fun experience to do that."

In spite of his positive years in the military, Wiegele recalls one negative aspect. "I always hated paydays. Well, not for myself, but for the poor kids that would get paid, and before they got their money there was a loan shark outside the door." He recalls those young soldiers asking him for loans. "I gave it to them for a while, but finally I had to say no." Wiegele admits many of them got into trouble gambling. Some, he says, were married, and their debts worried him. But with his own small salary and a wife at home, he could do little to help.

Looking back at the relationships he formed in the service, Wiegele regrets that he and his buddies haven't stayed in touch over the years. For a while, he got postcards from a few of them. His good friend,

Continued on page 130

Vietnam

WILLIAM OVERHOLSER
Lieutenant Colonel
US ARMY

Vietnam

WILLIAM OVERHOLSER
Spokane, Washington

In 1958, $27 a month for a part-time job was good money. That's what William Overholser earned when he moved from Basic ROTC to Advanced ROTC after two years at the University of Idaho. Added to that, his $30 monthly athletic scholarship and a small income from a "hashing" job in a sorority house provided for his needs at the University of Idaho.

Originally, Overholser had no plans for a military career. ROTC was easy income for him—especially the summer camp. "I was on a track scholarship," he explains, "so the summer camp was a piece of cake for me. All I had to do was yell loud and run fast. ROTC summer camp was kind of like basic training with not quite as much harassment, so I came out of there as a distinguished graduate."

As a result, he was recommended for a Regular Army commission and a three-year obligation. Also, he got his first choice of assignment: Germany. But because of issues involving the erection of the Berlin Wall, he couldn't take flight training as scheduled. He did complete the infantry officers' basic course, airborne training and ranger training. He was assigned to the Third Armored Division, whose mission was to plug the Fulda Gap, where the Soviet tank divisions were expected to invade Western Europe. He had married his college sweetheart, Marilyn Wylie, and she and the first of four sons would join him in Germany later.

Returning to the States in 1964, Overholser attended flight school, including fixed and rotary wing training. In September, 1965, he was assigned to Vietnam and served in an assault helicopter company, A company, 82nd Airborne Aviation whose workhorse was the UH 1 "Huey."

Soon afterwards, he attained the rank of captain. In his company he was one of fifty pilots, along with 350 enlisted men and 31 helicopters—plus all the support for company-level maintenance. They were initially stationed for three months in the French city of Vung Tau on the South China Sea. Then the unit moved to Bien Hoa, the main air base.

Looking back, Overholser states, "I'm proud to say that I was in A Company of the 82nd Airborne Division Aviation Company. There were a lot of gung-ho people around me; and I was gung-ho, too. I was with the top guys—paratroopers—and really dedicated soldiers, including the pilots. We were supporting the 173rd Airborne Brigade, which contained several infantry battalions. Most of the fighting then was across the river in War Zone D, to which they were flown in our choppers."

A typical day in Vietnam started with a 4 a.m. wake-up. After breakfast and a final briefing a flight of ten Hueys and two or three gunships would take off to pick up the Infantry troops. But during their months in Vung Tau, Overholser says, the daily job contrasted too much with the night life of the former French tourist town on the South China Sea. "It was surreal—emotionally loaded—to be in combat seeing death and destruction and then come back to this little French city with neon lights and taverns. Pilots would get out

Continued on page 130

ROBERT MECHAM
Major
US ARMY

Vietnam

ROBERT MECHAM
Spokane, Washington

When Bob Mecham graduated from Northwestern Dental School in 1962, he didn't remain a civilian for long. "At that time," he recalls, "the Vietnam thing was getting pretty warm, and any graduates of medical school or dental school either enlisted or would be drafted within a matter of months, so there really was no choice."

Older than most draftees, Mecham was already married with a child when he enlisted in the Army. He and his wife, Rita, hoped they'd be shipped to the Seattle area, where he could take his board dentistry exams. But when Mecham got a phone call, telling him to pack for Fort Lawton, he misunderstood. "Not knowing anything about Army procedures, I thought he meant Fort Lewis. I told everybody I was going to Fort Lewis, but I was lucky enough to go to the small Army hospital at Fort Lawton, Seattle." He didn't complain. "Fort Lawton was considered to be, at that time, the second-nicest place that you could spend a couple years in the U.S. Army. The other was the Presidio in California."

His main duty at the hospital involved preparing soldiers for service in Vietnam. "We spent a lot of time working on individuals or lieutenants from West Point that were heading over," he recalls. "Things were very, very busy." During his two-year hitch at Lawton, he served the dental needs of Army, Air Force and Navy personnel.

He says he enjoyed his work there, but he remembers one period in 1962-'63, when unrelated tragedies impacted him. "I got a notice that my best friend and best man at our wedding was killed at Guantanamo Bay, the day the Cuban missile crisis started." He says his friend crashed in a KC-135.

While still grieving over that loss, Mecham was hit with another sorrow: President Kennedy's assassination. During that November day of shock and mourning, he recalls an odd occurrence. "One of the commanding officers in the hospital, when he heard of the assassination, turned to a junior officer and said, 'What do you think this will do to the stock market?' The junior officer jumped all over the senior officer for thinking of that when we'd just lost a beloved president."

In 1964 Mecham left Fort Lawton, transferring to the 385th Hospital Unit in Spokane, Washington, as a member of the Army Reserve. He says he enjoyed those years, which were "actually a wonderful experience." He participated in medical units for the World Boy Scout Jamboree and the U.S. Boy Scout Jamboree. "These were wonderful opportunities for education," he recalls. Also, he attended various training classes at Walter Reed Hospital in Washington, D.C.; and Letterman General Hospital in San Francisco.

Certain memories from those hospital visits remain vivid for Mecham. "A lot of the amputees were sent to Letterman General for prosthetics and rehab," he says. "I'll tell you, when you saw many of those kids with no legs and no arms in high spirits, and guys carrying them down to the local watering hole to have a beer, you know they were tough. They were good. It made you proud."

Continued on page 132

BENJAMIN WHITE
E-7
US MARINE CORPS

Vietnam

BENJAMIN WHITE
Priest River, Idaho

Remembering a dramatic period in his military life, Benjamin White says, "I was privileged to spend 54 days with a broken back on the floor of the jungle during monsoon season. I was cold and wet with no fire and no friends." He uses the word "privileged," because of what he learned: "Of all the ways there are to die, I will not starve to death. I found that I could eat just about anything if it didn't eat me first."

With a cynical smile he adds, "That includes raw tiger."

He'd broken his back while parachuting into the area, but he kept his rifle handy. When the tiger approached, he recalls, it crouched eight feet from him. But White's terror served him well. He fired half a magazine of which only half dozen rounds hit the tiger. "I tell people that the tiger and I were going to have a meeting of the minds over lunch. But he lost his mind and became lunch." Because the enemy would easily locate White if he built a fire, he couldn't cook his meat. But that was fine because, he admits, "I didn't eat the tiger. I just tasted him."

Even so, the memory of that dangerous moment stays with him. "I still have a hard time getting along with cats."

A couple of years before the tiger incident, White had entered the Marine Corps, and in late 1960 he landed in Southeast Asia. He and many others thought they were prepared for anything, but the field training surprised even the toughest of them.

An officer grabbed a bullhorn and announced, "My name is Lieutenant Colonel Black. When I give you the word I want you to follow me. Leave your gear where it is." With that, he turned toward the trail. White recalls a unique marking on the back of the man's shirt. "It was two lines of writing. The first line said, 'Follow me,' and the second said, 'Keep up if you can.'" About 5000 people fell in after the lieutenant colonel, but when they finished the training, the number had dwindled to a mere 165.

"That was the only time I ran 44 miles in a single day in my life," White says.

Half-way into the run, they stopped for food and water. White and others grabbed bread and slabs of steak for sandwiches. After an hour and forty-five minutes Lieutenant Colonel Black ordered them up and moving. "We weren't expecting that," White says. "We thought the run was over."

In spite of the grueling training, White still has high regard for that colonel. "He was the epitome of a leader. He never asked us to do anything that he wasn't willing to do or hadn't done. He was about 6'1" and 170 pounds—just tougher than leather."

White doesn't say exactly where this training took place. He can't even say with certainty that he was in Vietnam—then or in the months that followed. Because the Vietnam conflict wouldn't begin for another three years, White's unit was in the area unofficially. "Our president later said we don't have any people there," he

Continued on page 132

~ 65 ~

VIRGIL JOE
Private First Class
US ARMY

Vietnam

VIRGIL JOE
Spokane, Washington

After boot camp in 1968, Virgil Joe accepted a variety of assignments—like communications and truck driving—before finding his niche in the kitchen.

As a cook, he says, he benefitted from the military in numerous ways. In fact, he believes one of the most valuable lessons involved making decisions. "I know how to take command," he contends. "So, when everybody else's saying, 'Well, I don't know,' that's where I come in." In his civilian life afterwards, he says, employers respected him because of this capability. "I could take charge and get the job done."

But the road hasn't always been easy. A year after enlisting, Joe was shipped to Vietnam and assigned to the 630th Combat Engineers. His first impression of the area? "Heat, humidity and the smell," he recalls. "These hit you when you get out of that DC-10. We arrived at midnight and the humidity was 180. You could sit doing nothing and sweat's pouring out of your pores."

The 630th Unit moved frequently. "We were lucky if we were in one spot two weeks," Joe says. From Da Nang to Fu Bai and countless other stopovers, he traveled across the country. But no matter where the unit went, Joe's job remained the same. "I stayed in the mess hall that whole time." During some of his months in Vietnam, Joe was attached to other mobile units as well, including the 45th Group, the 1st Marine Division, and the 101st Airborn—also called the Big Red One.

Because of the mobility issues, Joe and his crew decided to ditch the canvas-and-frame tent in favor of a "mess hall on wheels." They adapted a flat-bed trailer that they could transport easily, and on short notice. This came in handy when they were attached to bridge-building units, which changed locations frequently.

Joe remembers quirky situations at meal times. For example, he says, they often had more people than expected at a meal, "because South Vietnamese soldiers would try to sneak into the mess line."

As a result, Joe had to assert himself. "Our officers always waited for the troops to eat. But once, an ARVN [Army of the Republic of Vietnam] officer jumped to the head of the line." Joe says he responded immediately: "No, no, no! You go to the back."

The officer didn't appreciate orders from an underling. Trying to communicate in spite of the language barrier, the man pointed to himself and said, "Captain."

Unfazed, Joe stated his own rank: "Private."

Thinking back now, Joe recalls, "He looked at me kind of funny, and I said, 'No, our boys eat first, and officers last, Captain.'" To make his point more convincing, Joe says, "I walked around, grabbed him by the back, turned him around and explained it to him. He understood."

Another instance involved Joe's explaining the eating schedule to an American officer. "We had a canvas curtain that stayed closed on the mess wagon while we got the meal ready," he recalls. One time the

Continued on page 133

DENNIS BURGI
E-5 Second Class
US NAVAL AIR

Vietnam

DENNIS BURGI
Nine Mile Falls, Washington

Dennis Burgi's wartime philosophy served him well as he worked on medical evacuations and other search-and-rescue missions. He says, "Personally, I wasn't interested in how many I could kill; I'd rather see how many I could save."

When drafted in 1967, Burgi chose the Navy and completed basic training in San Diego. He and a buddy filled out their dream sheets together. The friend wanted to see combat, but Burgi preferred the Mediterranean or somewhere on the East Coast—anywhere except Vietnam. However, in typical military fashion, the other guy spent his entire four years in Pensacola, while Dennis was shipped to Imperial Beach and then Vietnam.

Burgi endured a difficult boot camp. His NCO, he says, used him as a scapegoat for any and all complaints. "Like when I shaved it wouldn't be good enough for him. Or, he would come in and look at all the racks and tear mine apart and have me redo it." In an attempt to appease the man, Dennis got up at 3:30 every morning—an hour earlier than his buddies, "so I could shave closer and make my bunk better and stuff. That drove the officer nuts." But the new recruit quickly realized a benefit to his position. "I did make a lot of friends, because they knew; they understood. He'd make them do push ups because of my rack," but it didn't matter to the others. Their unit became a close-knit group.

Burgi received aviation electronics technician training in Memphis. Next, he went to Imperial Beach and was soon assigned to a combat helicopter squadron on the USS Kittyhawk in Vietnam. He served on board for ten months, returning a year later for another tour.

One of his daily jobs involved watching takes-offs and landings. He flew in a "plane guard" during launches. Describing the work, he says, "We could pick up a pilot that was having problems or had to eject. If they could get to the water, we would do the over-water rescues. That's what we were best trained in. Occasionally when they had a massive attack where they needed extra helicopters for med evacs, we'd go in and do those also."

He usually worked nights, which sometimes meant hours of down-time. But he stayed busy as an electronics technician when he wasn't flying. On really slow shifts, Burgi and his buddies played pinochle.

Thanks to his line of work, Dennis made friends. He says a rescued pilot often wanted to show gratitude. "If a pilot had to eject and you picked him up, the next time you go into port, he'd buy you a drink."

However, one time Burgi turned down drinks in favor of another activity. "I said, 'I wanna fly in one of your airplanes. I've never been in one of your Phantoms.' The grateful pilot agreed, and Dennis took a memorable ride. "That launch was something else!" he recalls. Afterwards, he told the pilot, "I never want to do that again!" Today he still admits, "That was one of the scariest times of my life. Give me my crummy little helicopter instead."

Continued on page 134

BEN CABILDO
Spec-5 Sergeant
US ARMY

Vietnam

BEN CABILDO
Medical Lake, Washington

Ben Cabildo, a Pilipino-American who served during the Vietnam years, sees war from a surprising perspective—for several reasons.

At age 14, Cabildo immigrated with his family from the Philippines to Seattle, where he graduated from high school in 1967. He enlisted and volunteered for a tour in Vietnam, he says, "without really knowing who the Communists were."

Boot camp offered him the opportunity to meet a variety of people from across the country, young men from farms and from inner cities. He grew to appreciate diversity. "It was really a great experience for me meeting all those people," he recalls. "It was just wonderful. I loved those kids."

Once deployed to Vietnam, Ben went to Long Than North-Bearcat, where he helped set up a headquarters for his company and served as a perimeter guard. But almost immediately he realized the danger of his position. "I didn't want to die young," he says. "So I read a message from the battalion saying they needed a logo for the company. Since I liked to design things, I designed the logo, and they awarded me an office job in Vung Tao City, which was like a resort." He believes that was a good move, because six months later the Long Than North area was taken by the enemy.

As a member of the 303rd Transportation Company, Ben worked in administration. He eventually served under the company commander of the transportation company with the Helicopter Battalion.

But he faced an unseen enemy during his time in Vietnam: prejudice among his own men. "There were issues of discrimination," he states. "There were a lot of times when minorities were discriminated against by both officers and enlisted men who didn't understand that we were all in it together. We all had to work side by side and protect each other."

He did his part in educating his buddies and preventing name-calling. One of his favorite lines was, "We must stick together and not divide ourselves from our mates." He recalls occasional fistfights stemming from racial or cultural prejudice. Still, when they realized the value of a united company, Cabildo believes most soldiers "became cool with it; and through the experience of working side by side, they really learned."

Cabildo's negotiating skills served him well. He often told fellow soldiers, "We are all Americans. Even though I look different, I am an American." As a result, he says, he made a lot of friends. Furthermore, "I learned from this experience how to explain things to people, which was an advantage when I got out of the military."

But another type of conflict arose—one which Cabildo could not negotiate away. While still in Vietnam, he says, "We were getting second-hand information saying that the people back home who were demonstrating didn't really know what was happening in Vietnam, that they were unpatriotic and anti-American. The media

Continued on page 136

~ 71 ~

RALPH DECRISTOFORO
Captain
US AIR FORCE

Vietnam

RALPH DECRISTOFORO
Spokane, Washington

When Ralph DeCristoforo considers his Air Force career, he believes he made the right decision to enlist. If not, what can he do about it now? "There are no do-overs in life," he says.

Born in inner-city Philadelphia in 1951, DeCristoforo and his family lived in a mixed neighborhood. His Italian-Ukrainian heritage offered him the opportunity to interact with people of various backgrounds. He recalls, "It was fun to grow up there."

But after high school, he couldn't find a satisfying career. "I kind of wandered around working," he says, but without purpose. He then applied to the Coast Guard Academy and passed all tests—except the color-vision exam. "That meant I couldn't be an officer, because officers had to read colored flags."

Before he could consider another branch of the service, the military draft was instituted. DeCristoforo's number was so low he couldn't find a good civilian job. Every prospective employer, he recalls, would ask, "What number are you in the lottery?" He realized a military career might be his only future, so he decided on the Air Force and joined in 1970, just after his 19th birthday.

"I had high marks on all the scores," he remembers, "but because of my color vision there wasn't much out there. Air Freight was the only thing." That was fine with him; he liked the idea of driving heavy equipment, preferring that to cooking or working security. But he learned from an instructor that the job wouldn't be easy. He recalls being told, "The death rate for your career field is high. There is a likelihood that they'll give you your rifle and a forklift and say, 'The drop zone is a quarter mile that way—go pick something up and bring it back.'" Upon hearing this, he says, "I wasn't feeling too good."

Nonetheless, after a few months of training, DeCristoforo was deployed overseas. He spent much of his tour in Japan, at an Air Force staging point for med-evacs coming out of Vietnam and Korea.

One memory stands out above all the rest.

"It was Christmas Eve, 1971, and a C5 came in; a C5 is the largest cargo carrier that the Air Force has," he explains. "We were told there were human remains on board. 'Home Runs,' we called them, the guys going home. They hit it. They're heading for home."

DeCristoforo remembers seeing the cargo door open. "The whole plane was full, top to bottom, front to back, with silver caskets." There were 36 pallets, and each pallet held 12 bodies. "They were all out of Vietnam and heading home." At that moment, he and fellow airmen stood silent, struck with the reality of war.

Now, four decades later, he says, "It's the first time I've been able to tell this."

Those weren't the only casualties DeCristoforo saw during his tour of duty. He believes, moreover, the official tallies might have been misleading to the public. Halfway through the Vietnam conflict, he says, the military changed their method of counting. "It was only listed as a fatality or KIA (killed in action) if the

Continued on page 137

DOUGLASS LIVINGSTONE
E-5
US ARMY

Vietnam

DOUGLASS LIVINGSTONE
Spokane, Washington

"It's always there; it intrudes, you know. There's never a day goes by I don't think something about it."

That's how Douglas Livingstone describes his life—forty years after he served in Vietnam. The memories still haunt him, with good reason. After a miserably cold boot camp in Fort Lewis, where many endured spinal meningitis and pneumonia, he was shipped to Camron Bay. There, he says, "It was so hot that it was like getting slapped in the face with a hot wet towel. It stunk, too; but you get used to that pretty quick." After a week of in-country training, he transferred to Fire Support Base west in the Que Son Valley, situated between Da Nang and Chu Lai. One of his main duties involved sweeping the jungles and valleys to provide security for the resettlement village of Hiep Duc.

He didn't mind the hot weather, but the enemy? "Sure, I was scared," he acknowledges. "They'd show me on a map where to go, and it was up to me to get there. These were search and destroy missions." Livingstone and his good friend Tracy both served as point men, and eventually they worked as a team in Alfa Company.

Having a partner he could trust helped his attitude, but he admits morale in general suffered. "We were given no explanation as to what we were doing. It felt like a loose-knit bunch of wackos stomping around in the brush. I was in the field 10 of my 14 months," he recounts. "The world turned upside down during that period in my life."

And, he believes, the soldiers' off-duty activities contributed to the problem. "After three days of stand-down, which were three days of boozing and pub-crawling, plus letter writing to sober up, it left us in worse shape when we went back than when we came out."

Making matters worse, Livingstone was injured and suffered complications. He remembers someone taking a shot at him, and "I tumbled ten feet through some elephant grass into a dry washout, wrenching my back. Several days later, when we went back to Chu Lai, I went to the doctor to have him look at my back. When I got there, my leg wouldn't bend. All the infection in my body centered on top of my knee cap."

The doctor drained the knee and ordered the company medic to dress it twice a day and keep it dry. Such care, however, wasn't likely under the circumstances. "Sure," Livingstone says sarcastically, "when you're in monsoon season passing through streams up to your neck. The thing got rotten bad, and I was giddy and losing it because of all the infection in my body." Fortunately, the medic realized the seriousness of his condition, and he persuaded the brass to transfer Livingstone.

"That," he says thankfully, "was the beginning of my career in the rear."

Livingstone saw his share of poor leadership, including one platoon commander, who wandered into enemy fire with only 20 days left in his second tour. Another—a second lieutenant—seemed intent on spit-and-polish military order. Standing on a bunker, this new officer assured his troops that; "I'm going to hump

Continued on page 137

THOMAS POFF
Private First Class
US MARINE CORPS

Vietnam

THOMAS POFF
"Iceman"
Coeur d'Alene, Idaho

Thomas Poff grew up in St. Louis. His father had been a machine gunner in World War II, and the son remembers him fondly. "My dad was the gentlest man ever," he says. "We played catch and built stairways and rock walls." Tragically, Mr. Poff died of a ruptured artery at age 44, and Thomas had a difficult time with grief and anger. "Something inside of me just died. I wanted to hurt everything in the world."

Football became an outlet for his emotions. "When my dad died," he recalls, "I didn't have much humanity left in me; to be quite honest, I hated everybody. In football, I got to hurt people." The contact sport and its physical exertion helped Poff, but he still missed his father. Even today he speaks highly of him. "I will never be a tenth of the man my dad was—never."

Football couldn't heal all of Poff's distress. After high school, he enlisted in the Marines. "My mom understood that I was a wild child," he says. "There are people out there who are wild. We can't help it."

Poff remembers basic training with a smile. "I was in great shape. Run five miles; eat breakfast; run five miles to digest. Then you go to exercise. Boot camp, yeah, I liked it."

His training served him well, and he eventually became part of a special unit: Force Recon. "I was picked," he says, "because I was the best of the best. I could run a six-minute mile with a rifle and a 50-pound pack on my back. I did three miles in 18 minutes flat. I'm proud of that."

His nickname, "Iceman," came about because of his dependability. "What had to be done, you called me," he asserts. "No matter where it was. It was my job. My captain one time said, 'I don't know how he does it; he must have ice in his veins.' That's how I got the name."

Thinking back on his days in Vietnam, he recalls the unpleasant surroundings. For example, he warns, "Bugs were a killer; never sleep next to a tree. Centipedes were 10 to 12 inches long. They could take a bite out of you the size of a nickel, and that's no lie." Ants posed an additional problem. If five or six of them bit, he says, it felt like getting hit by a bullet.

Weather in Southeast Asia also contributed to his misery. "Monsoon season wasn't all that great," Poff recalls. He and fellow Marines used condoms to cover the tops of their gun barrels, to keep them dry on the inside.

"I used an M14-7.62 round," he says. "That was a heavy rifle. Fully loaded it weighed 9.5 pounds." He preferred the M-14 , which could function in any situation. "You can throw it in the mud, dripping mud and then empty the clip. If you threw an M16 in the mud, picked it up and pulled the trigger, all you'd hear is 'click.' President Johnson's people were too cheap to send a cleaning kit with each M-16."

As a sniper, Poff was often inserted into an area from a helicopter. "I jumped out first because I was in charge," he says.

Continued on page 138

JOE RICHART
Corporal E-4
US ARMY

Vietnam

JOE RICHART
Colville, Washington

Drafted in 1970, Joe Richart finished boot camp and took advanced MP training at Fort Gordon. Soon after arriving in Vietnam he made a startling discovery: "When you go to Nam—I don't care who you are—you're cannon fodder." Even though Joe himself didn't succumb to a cannon, he says the year he spent in combat "was enough to make me go crazy."

Looking back, he points to two disturbing aspects of Vietnam. First, he mentions the dumping of Agent Orange. "They come over you one day about daylight and it feels just like some stinky horse piss is raining on you. If you survived through that day and daylight the next day, all vegetation and most of the wildlife around the area was dead. It denuded the landscape and it looked like the after-effects of a forest fire."

Also troubling, he says, was the effect of the conflict on the Vietnamese kids. He can still see them in his mind's eye. "They would run around half-naked and dirty, tears running down their face, scared out of their wits. It was just plain horrifying," he says, admitting the Americans could do little for them. The situation "just ripped our guts out."

In spite of these difficulties, Richart completed his tour and returned to the States. But he didn't make an easy transition. "The debriefing in those days when I came back was to stop at a military depot to get a shower, a set of greens, a hot meal, and a ticket to home," he says. "That took about 24 hours. But that was not enough time to unwind. I was having nightmares and I felt that I would just as soon shoot somebody as look at them. I saw that was not conducive to civilized living."

When he arrived in Seattle, he visited with parents and grandparents—and with a brother who'd recently returned from a tour in Germany. Unfortunately, the siblings' military experiences differed so much they seemed to have little in common. "But," Joe says, "that changed after he went through conflict at Desert Storm. We're still brothers. We won't let anyone else pick on the other. We stand up for each other."

After the family visit, Joe chose a remote location for a long-term debriefing: Kettle Falls, Washington, where his father owned 240 acres of timberland. "I spent about three years out there in the brush by myself. My grandparents and three uncles lived on their ranch at the top of the hill about five miles away. They knew I didn't want to be bothered, but they knew I couldn't stay out there by myself."

As a compromise, the family left notes hanging on Joe's locked gate, instructing him about upcoming jobs. He'd read the notes, do the work—such as mending fences—and post a reply. Later he'd go back to the spot and find payment in the form of money, tobacco or "maybe a pack of grub that they had left for me."

Eventually, he says, "I felt good enough and comfortable enough to come back and stay with some people." But life did not automatically become easier. Several more years would pass before he sought assistance.

Continued on page 139

PAT BIGGS
Midshipman ~ US NAVY
Captain ~ US ARMY

Vietnam

PAT BIGGS
Spokane, Washington

One year at Annapolis showed Pat Biggs a side of military life he didn't like. Referring to that experience as a "365 day boot camp without respite," Biggs recounts what he calls sadistic treatment of some plebes by some, well-known, upper classmen. He recalls an instance where a classmate drew especially negative attention with his admission he did not recognize the name of Babe Ruth. After weeks of ridicule, sleep deprivation and physical harassment, that plebe leaped to his death from a tower on the campus.

He nevertheless also has positive memories of the Naval Academy experience, such as a fleeting friendship with classmate Roger Staubach, the thrill of marching in formation before visitors. "I did have the pleasure" he says, and "of feeling the esprit of marching to military music, to the drums, in spotless dress uniforms, synchronized, before the admiring eyes of visitors."

Deciding that a Navy career was a poor fit, he left Annapolis after one year, and in 1962 at age eighteen, he transferred to the University of Washington. This was a period when the military draft was constantly on the mind of persons his age. After a few months in the Navy Reserve, he joined the Army ROTC program where he recalls, over the years leading to active duty in 1970, he participated in a variety of required training events which he describes as all similar to the boot camp experience at Annapolis. ROTC Summer Camp, Officer's Basic, Army Signal School occurred here and there in summer months.

Biggs does not look back with favor on those training camp experiences. He has come to view them as "just chuckholes to pass through." He developed a "private contempt" for these relentlessly authoritarian environments that" inflated the highers and threatened the lowers."

Explaining this attitude, he offers detailed responses: "with each boot camp, we had to repeat these search and capture, low crawl through a firing range, run in place with a rifle held perpendicular to the body, locked in a footlocker pounded by baseball bats, pull ups before meals, herded into bleachers at midnight in freezing weather to be instructed on how to kill another human with piano wire; heat, humidity, dust, all the standard-issue man stuff."

He reviews these times and the many chuckholes he was required to pass through, notices the many others who never experienced any chuckholes thrown in front of them, and notes that those chuckholes were encountered along a way that he sees as imposed, hardly chosen. He believes the years of passing through these repetitive events encouraged a childhood tendency to split off, to withdraw emotionally from highly charged situations, and to role play what was required to meet social expectations. He believes his Vietnam era service, from 1962 to 1971, and the consequences of that service have been a primary factor in a series of tragic events in the years that followed. He is discouraged about the prospect that the world will ever be free of fat old men

Continued on page 139

LARRY SCOTT
E-4
US ARMY AIRBORNE

Vietnam

LARRY SCOTT
Hayden Lake, Idaho

The only time Larry Scott ever won a lottery, he says, was in 1970. That's when his number was a very low 11 and he got a draft notice.

After boot camp, he took infantry training. "I really enjoyed getting out and firing the weapons, map reading, and all the classes they put you through," he recalls. He then took three weeks of mortar training, followed by another three weeks of infantry. "Unfortunately, during my final days of instruction, I suffered a lower-leg stress fracture. So," he says, "I ended up in clerical school in Fort Leonard Wood, Missouri. I hated it. I didn't like sitting behind a desk poking a typewriter. I never did learn how to type."

Eventually, he went to Vietnam anyway—with the 101st Airborne Infantry. "When I got there, they put me in what they call tactical operations, which I enjoyed." His job involved plotting troop movement in the field, and he had a highly classified clearance. In addition, every six days he traveled to remote locations to deliver the troops' mail. Under such circumstances, he faced frequent danger. "Sometimes I would get stuck out in the field," he remembers. "We were hit quite a few times by mortars and enemy fire."

But generally, he didn't allow himself to be afraid. "The only time you really get nervous is when reality sets in," he says. "And you think, hey, this isn't a cool place. Somebody is trying to kill me. You're out there where your life is on the line, and you realize it's do or die."

Like many infantrymen, Scott knew the chain of command didn't always correspond to bars on uniforms. He believes lieutenants new to combat often deferred to their sergeants in the field. In fact, he contends, "High rank officers were usually out there just to get rank or their overseas medals and stuff. They were there for six months, just long enough to get a commendation, Silver Star, or whatever, and they were gone."

As a result, enlisted men showed little respect toward some officers. One example proves his point. When a new colonel took command, he immediately called for an inspection of the troops. Dirty, bedraggled soldiers standing in formation in the middle of a war zone? Scott still remembers the officer's command: "Tomorrow morning you will be out here in starched fatigues and shined boots!"

Of course, many infantrymen resented the order, and Scott says, "They thought this guy needed to be educated. That night they popped a C.S. Gas grenade outside of his hooch, blocked his door, and sat out there laughing when the colonel was trying to beat the doors down to get out of his hooch."

Scott smiles at the memory. "That colonel didn't have his Class-A inspection the next day nor his starched fatigues."

Scott remembers one date in great detail—December 11, 1970, his 21st birthday. "My buddies wanted me to go to an N.C.O. Club at Battalion. They felt I needed to get drunk on my 21st. I wasn't a drinker. I told them maybe later. That night someone threw a hand grenade in the back door of the club. 28 men were

Continued on page 140

PHIL WHITE
Spec 4 E-4
US ARMY
Combat Medic

Vietnam

PHIL WHITE
Spokane, Washington

Even though he originally had no plans for the military, Phil White said he joined anyway—and with the wrong motivation. "I was a veterinary medicine student in my freshman year in college," he says, but he didn't care for the rigors of academics.

When Army recruiters visited his campus, he felt the appeal. "These guys come up in their jump boots and all their little doodads on their chest, and their green beret," he recalls. "They are all massive men and they are looking good. They talk sweet and say, 'All you have to do is give us another year and you could be a green beret, too.' And I said, 'Take me.' In the back of my head I was like, 'Oh, the women will love this. I'll get girls hanging off of me.'"

He now admits, "That didn't happen."

After volunteering in 1968, White went to boot camp at Fort Ord, California. "Basic training was great," he recalls. "I was an athlete—a track guy right out of high school." But he had a tough drill instructor. "I swore if I saw him in Vietnam I would shoot him. That's not true now. As you get older you kind of realize what they were trying to do, and some of the stuff he taught me kept me alive."

When he finished at Fort Ord, he hoped to pursue some area of veterinary work in the Army. He knew of a meat inspector position, and he'd heard that someone was assigned to oversee the General's pets. But the Army had other plans, and White became a combat medic. He attended medical school, jump school and Special Forces training.

Then he went to Vietnam.

Assigned to the AmeriCal Division, he quickly discovered the acute need for medics in the field. "That was right after the Tet Offensive of '68," he says, "and all of the medics were decimated."

His duties involved considerable danger. "We would go into a village and evacuate that village of indigenous people, helicopter them out. Then we'd leave for a couple of days, evacuate another village, and come back to that original village. Anybody that was back in there was VC or NVA. They were always shooting at us when we came back. We didn't know which of them was friend or enemy. Unfortunately, you have to consider everybody your enemy."

White understands the negative aspects of combat. He states, "War is not fun. It's not meant to be fun. Sometimes I question whether it's necessary." However, he pauses and considers the pros and cons, concluding that war can prevent certain people from usurping power. "We would have maybe another Hitler or Mussolini, and we don't want that."

Soon after arriving in Vietnam, White discovered his officers' strict adherence to rules—particularly those dealing with controlled substances. He explains, "I was the CO's medic, so when he introduced himself,

Continued on page 141

RALPH NOLL
Spec 4
US ARMY

Vietnam

RALPH NOLL
Spokane, Washington

Prior to being drafted Ralph suffered several injuries that ended his wrestling scholarship to Olympia College. He was still in the healing stage from surgeries to his shoulders and knees, a shattered wrist and concussion, when he received his draft notice. At that period of the Viet Nam War the military did not discriminate between men that were not fit for duty and those that were. They were taking every man. The medical evidence was ignored and Ralph was inducted and subsequently sent to Viet Nam. The injuries he had before he was drafted were exacerbated by basic training and serving in combat.

Ralph was not prepared for the reality of Viet Nam. He said when the doors of the plane opened he could smell smoke, stench, diesel and oppressive heat. The sky was a brown smog. The first night in Danang there was a rocket attack. The Viet Cong attempted to infiltrate. The enemy had the strategy of attacking in the early morning hours. The matters of war were complicated by the conflicts going on between the American soldiers—the black men and the white men, the soldiers and the officers. Two sergeants and one captain were fragged the same night Ralph arrived in country.

The next day Ralph was on a plane to Phu Bi. From there he boarded a duce and half to Camp Eagle. Ralph rememberes, " All night the Viet Cong were hitting us with rockets and mortars. The tension within the camp was at a fever pitch. There was the real enemy we came to fight, but all the time there was the bitterness between blacks and whites and the hatred of some officers by their men. Everybody had to watch their back. If you were white you may die at the hands of a black. If you were black the reverse was true. If you were an officer you better watch everybody. No one could relax and the situation made everyone nuts."

One night Charlie hit hard around 3 a.m. Ralph was in his underwear and made a run for the bunker. Everybody was running a screaming "incoming." A rocket hit and Ralph was blown through the air. He didn't know if he was alive because everything turned surreal. He was flying and reaching but there was nothing there. When he hit, he hit hard. He couldn't get up because the ground was vibrating. When he managed to get to his feet the explosions continued to knock him around as he made a fast crawl to the bunker and dove in head first. He became cold and clammy and began throwing up. He was in shock.

"After the attack we made our way back to the company," Ralph says. He didn't know he was injured until someone helped him get to the dispensary. The sergeant wanted him to get back to his company, but the doctor was a captain and ordered the sergeant out of the dispensary until he finished dressing Ralph's injuries. By noon the next day Ralph was on his way to Dong Ha, a mile from the DMZ. He was stationed there until it was time for him to go home.

When Ralph arrived home he expected to pick up where he left off. He dreamed about coming home and going back to college and making contact with his friends and seeing his family. He found he could not

Continued on page 143

CRAIG MONTGOMERY
Spec 4
US ARMY

Vietnam

CRAIG MONTGOMERY
Spokane, Washington

Growing up in the Northwest, Craig Montgomery loved to hunt, but not to kill. "I lined up on elk a few times but never told my father because I didn't pull the trigger," he says. "I just didn't want to. I was amazed at how large they were and how beautiful." His father, an avid sportsman, couldn't understand that Craig was more fascinated by the animals' majesty than their meat.

After attending Lewis & Clark College, he enlisted and enjoyed basic training at Fort Leonard Wood. "It was repetitious," he recalls, "and I liked sports. I'd played all sports and excelled in them—football, basketball, baseball, track. I was in real good shape."

Soon he was shipped to Vietnam, where his unit built fighting bunkers—70 feet long and 25-30 feet wide—in which the troops slept. He also helped construct guard bunkers and cook shacks. For a year the unit worked to set up three base camps. But Montgomery knew Agent Orange had been sprayed near one of the camps. "We moved into this area and when we took a break I could smell this stench. I never smelled anything like that in my life. At first I thought it was a sewer disposal."

While he'll always remember that foul odor, another smell made an even stronger impression on him. "I saw this little burned area, and it looked like a crater, and I knew a bomb had hit there." When he went to investigate, he discovered all vegetation and wildlife around the crater had died.

But what he found at the bottom of the hole was even worse. "I walked right up to the edge and saw a mass of people. They were burned and decayed." Montgomery says the memory will never go away. "Even now if something smells, that's where my mind goes, and I can see that picture for a week or two."

In addition to repulsive sights and odors, Montgomery faced constant danger. During a convoy, he noticed three Vietnamese civilians carrying bundles of bamboo shoots on the road ahead of them. Two of the bundles were 10-12 feet long, but the third was considerably shorter. When the locals saw military vehicles approaching, they dropped their bundles onto the road. "Suspicious activity," Montgomery remembers thinking, so he hollered, "Bamboo pipe bomb!"

The small pickup truck in which he rode stopped, and he and his buddy Morris jumped out, scampering around to the back. But the five-ton truck behind them didn't stop in time. "All I heard was a bang," Montgomery says. "I hit the back of my neck and head and the small of my back on the tailgate. I was out like a light." In the process, though, he somehow managed to pull his friend to safety—an amazing feat, considering Montgomery weighed 155 and Morris topped the scales at 245.

Thanks to Montgomery's quick thinking, Morris survived, but he sustained an injury. When Montgomery regained consciousness, he saw him, "lying there with his fingers clipped off. The next thing I knew, this

Continued on page 144

CRAIG THOMAS
Private First CLass
US ARMY

Vietnam

CRAIG THOMAS
Spokane, Washington

At the time, Craig Thomas didn't realize the value of his Boy Scout training, or of hunting trips with his dad, or even of high school sports. But all those activities played an important part in preparing him for Vietnam. "I was in good shape," he says. "And, I knew how to handle weapons and enjoy the outdoors. I knew how to hike and what was expected of me out in the woods."

Thomas got his draft notice after graduation in 1967 and completed boot camp in Fort Lewis, Washington. Later, at Fort Carson, Colorado, he joined C Company, 1st Battalion of the 11th Infantry, 5th Mechanized Infantry Division, as a rifleman, and his unit was deployed to the Quang Tri Province of Vietnam.

Three months and 28 days later, he was wounded.

His job at Quang Tri, situated on the DMZ, had made him "an easy target," he says. He carried a 15-pound PRICK-25 radio—complete with antenna—on his back and an M16 on his shoulder while conducting search-and-destroy missions. At night, his unit swept the jungles around Con Thien, Khe-Sahn and Quang Tri itself. They even entered the DMZ to destroy hidden bunkers and ammunition dumps.

Fortunately, Craig recalls, "We had a really good company commander. He knew how to keep us out of the trouble." Thomas' unit felt relatively safe. "We had only a couple guys get killed before I got wounded," he recalls.

He also notes the deep relationships he formed. "We were good friends. We were a band of brothers," he says. "I remember them all." Most of his buddies hailed from the Midwest, but one—Terry Patton—shared Craig's home state of Washington. Because of that, "We wrote Dan Evans, then governor of Washington, and asked for a state flag, because we were on the line from the moment we got there. Dan Evans actually sent us one." Everyone in the platoon signed the flag, and one of the soldiers later brought it home.

In spite of the friendships, Thomas and his buddies felt uncomfortable about being in Vietnam. "I knew the first day, the first morning, that we didn't belong there. There was something wrong with the whole thing. Someone's been lying to us." The young fighters at times wondered what they were fighting for. Looking back, Craig says, "Basically we were kids, you know, 20 years old. I was never a history buff. I look at Vietnam as an experience, okay? That's all. If you try to dwell on it and try to either criticize or rationalize, you will go crazy. You can't do it."

October 2, 1968, began like most other days—with combat on the front lines. Thomas' unit, assaulting a bunker position, had been in a fire fight for a day and a half. He and his buddies walked the ridge line, to capture an enemy bunker position, in support of B Company, which had taken excessive hits from the enemy. Before he could fully analyze the situation and assess the damage, he heard an explosion. "My right leg was blown off below the knee," he says. Lying in elephant grass, he wondered for a moment what had happened. "I

Continued on page 145

DALE GUDMUNSON
Seaman Recruit
US COAST GUARD

1950 ~ 2008

Vietnam

DALE GUDMUNSON
Colfax, Washington

Julie Eide describes her father, Dale Gudmunson, as a man of "very high intelligence"—but easily bored. After high school he wanted to expand his horizons and "see what else life had to offer," she says. "He wanted to work with his hands, do something productive and meaningful. He wanted to learn a trade and be successful."

To satisfy these ambitions, Gudmunson considered the Coast Guard. When a longtime friend joined, he followed suit. Unfortunately, though, he was injured during boot camp. A bad landing when scaling a wall resulted in a wrenched knee and a partial disability. But the accident didn't eliminate him from the service. "He was placed into the communications field and sent to school," Julie explains. "He was a seaman recruit in the Transportation Division of the United State Coast Guard. He served in Communications as a radioman in New York."

After the military, Gudmunson frequently relied on his Coast Guard training in electronics and communications. Julie says, "He used the knowledge so many times in his field of construction throughout his life." He owned and operated a construction company with his father and two brothers in Colfax, Washington, for 25 years. In 1992, he moved to Spokane and established another business, Exterior Concepts, which he operated until 1995 when he had a stroke. He remained in the construction field as a consultant and designer..

"The Coast Guard offered him the opportunity to prove to himself that he could accomplish whatever he set his mind to do," Julie adds. "He was very proud to have served in the military." He strongly supported the idea of defending Americans' freedoms.

Like many military personnel, Gudmunson got a tattoo. His daughter says he never explained his motivation, beyond the fact that "everyone was getting a tattoo in the service, so he wanted one, too." In the years that followed, it constantly reminded him of his military experiences.

Sadly, Dale Gudmunson passed away in 2008, shortly after meeting the artist at the VA Medical Center in Spokane. Though he sat for the portrait, he didn't have the opportunity to see the finished product.

National Defense Service Medal

GREG L. LAMBERT
Spec 4
US ARMY

Vietnam

GREG L. LAMBERT
Nine Mile Falls, Washington

When Greg Lambert's unit landed in Saigon in 1968, he says, "I knew what we were in for, because the runway on both sides was stacked with bodies."

Whether the corpses were Vietnamese or Americans, it didn't matter. Either way, Lambert remembers, "It put the fear of God into me right there."

He joined the 9th Unit at the village of Tan Tru, and almost immediately encountered a health problem. "I got what they call jungle rot on my legs," he says. "It was pretty bad." After several days of recovery, he returned to the battlegrounds. But he shouldn't have. Walking through rice paddies worsened his condition. "The sores would just eat into your flesh, some times clear to the bone. At the dispensary, every day, they'd take a cotton swab with peroxide and clean those wounds. Then they'd take a GI brush, medicate us, and scrub our legs," he explains. "It was painful."

Years later, he still bears the scars.

Lambert's mission involved search and destroy. To do this, his unit went on Eagle flights during the days and boat excursions at night. The intense, emotionally draining work affected everyone, who often spoke of surviving to fight another day. Lambert, like the others, assumed a kill-or-be-killed attitude, and he served doggedly for six months. But then something happened to alter his future.

He got a call from the Red Cross.

"I had a wife and a baby at home," he says, "and my wife was leaving the baby in the bar and takin' off and stuff like that." The Red Cross called him home on emergency leave, because no one was available to feed and care for the baby girl. Lambert returned to the States, but he had trouble making the mental and emotional shift. "Here I am, coming from a war zone directly into takin' care of an eight-month-old baby. My mind-set was killing people; and then the next day I'm raising a baby," he muses. He'd hoped to make a career in the military, but his superiors recommended that he get out because of the family hardship.

He knew he'd need a job. "I can thank the military for giving me a sense of responsibility," he says. "I learned to be self-motivated." He got training as a machinist and found work at Boeing, where he stayed for 20 years.

But throughout that time, something wasn't right. Latent feelings from Vietnam often surfaced. Lambert pushed them aside, but eventually they'd reappear. "I got to the point where I wanted to kill my boss. I was ready to choke him, physically," he says. He went to a VA doctor and said, "I gotta get out of here." Making an appointment the next day with a VA psychiatrist should have helped. She asked him about depression and anxiety, and about his experiences in Vietnam. "But I didn't want to talk about that stuff," he admits. "These people wouldn't understand."

Continued on page 146

RAY
Private First Class
US ARMY

Date of Service 1968 ~ 1971
Vietnam

RAY
Leggett, California

Ray, who requests that his last name not be used, says, "I don't want anybody to get me wrong, I have a lot of friends that were in the military and served in Vietnam. I have nothing against military people who put their life in jeopardy. But what I have feelings about are people who put others in jeopardy for no reason except to further their own military career."

He noticed that often during his time in the service. "I was pretty gung-ho at first," he asserts, "but I saw how the system worked and didn't care for it. I didn't think it was a good way to serve my country."

Ray's attitude stemmed from America's involvement in Vietnam. "We were being shuffled through as fast as we could be shuffled, so they could get us over there. A lot of the people who were destined to be cannon fodder were the poor and uneducated; that's where I felt it wasn't right."

He responded by going AWOL.

Other concurring events played a role in his decision. He'd wanted to fly helicopters, so he took the test. "I was one of the lucky ones who passed," he says, and he would've taken the training except for one problem: "We found out a very disturbing thing, that I'm terrified of heights. That canceled me out." Instead, he was put in advanced infantry training, which didn't suit him at all. "The last thing I wanted in the military was to be cannon fodder."

So, Ray and a friend hatched a plan. "When the chow truck brought in the chow," he says, "we jumped in the back. We changed to civilian clothes, went into Seattle, and got a Greyhound Bus out of there." The friend and Ray parted ways, and Ray headed for his childhood home in Northern California. But his freedom didn't last long. "I was picked up by the sheriff's department, who recognized that I was AWOL," and they shipped him to the Presidio for processing.

But during the paperwork shuffle, Ray somehow managed to sneak out a back window. He hitched a ride across the Golden Gate Bridge and traveled north again. Soon afterward, he was apprehended and returned to the Presidio. He tried the same stunt again—and again. "This went on about eight times," he remembers. "After the fifth or sixth time, they got pretty tired of me."

Ray tried to convince the authorities that he'd be satisfied with a dishonorable discharge, but he says that made them more determined to punish him. With each return to the Presidio, he got worse treatment.

"In the morning they would get you up and you would do calisthenics until you were so tired you could hardly stand up, and then they would let you eat breakfast standing at attention. You would go out in the afternoon to pick up garbage, and you went with a shotgun guard." He says when he fell into bed, extremely exhausted, the guards would rattle tin cups on the cell bars all night.

Ray remembers one of his fellow prisoners, a man he calls "T," who had trash duty one day. "T asked the guy that was guarding him, 'What would you do if I ran?'"

Continued on page 146

Post Vietnam

Desert Storm

Iraq

GARY BARTON
RM-3
US NAVY

Date of Service 1975 ~ 1979

GARY BARTON
Mesa, Arizona

Referring to his decision to enlist in 1975, Gary Barton says, "The most profound thing was the weight that I felt lifted, getting out of Spokane into a whole new world. Everything from the past was behind me; it was a brand new start, which was the paramount thing about my enlistment."

Flying into San Diego, Barton and several other recruits waited at the airport for a military bus to the base. He vividly recalls the Marine shuttle, which arrived first. "This guy came stomping out of the bus yelling and screaming and pointing, barking out orders like a mad man. He got all of the Marine recruits on the bus and off they went." Barton looked at his Navy buddies and wondered, "Holy socks, what did we get ourselves into?"

Moments later, when the Navy bus showed up, they expected more of the same. But Barton and his fellow recruits looked at the bus in disbelief. "It appeared old and gray, and needed a wax job bad with the paint quite oxidized. There was a bearded guy in dungarees driving, and he said, 'Come on, guys, let's go.'"

The driver pointed out some hot spots, for liberty, on the way. They didn't reach the base until midnight. After visiting the clinic for inoculations, they fell into bed in the wee hours. But their rest was cut short: "Up at five in the morning, to the sound of crashing trash cans, and our day started. It was the longest day of my life."

Not all recruits fared well in boot camp. In fact, Barton believes only about 20 of the original 80 in his company completed basic training as scheduled. Some couldn't take the physical endurance. "There were tests all the time," Barton says, "and if you didn't pass, they set you back." But he made it through, because he "was young, determined, and in pretty good shape."

Afterwards, he took fleet training and transferred to the Mediterranean, aboard the USS *Inchon*. That's when he experienced the first of several mishaps.

As a part of the refueling crew early in his deployment, Barton stood near the bulkhead of the helicopter carrier. He watched as his ship hooked to another to refuel. At first, the process went smoothly.

Then chaos erupted.

"Horns started blowing," he recalls. "We ducked down and the chief came running, dumping everything in the water—all of the lines, the hoses, everything. 'Get out of here!' he yelled. There must have been 50 guys on the refueling crew." Everyone made it inside the ship. Within seconds the two ships collided, and the crew grabbed onto whatever they could, hoping not to be knocked down in the jolt.

But the collision could have been worse. Barton says an equipment malfunction caused the other ship to scrape the side of his carrier. "Rumor had it that the rudder on the other ship malfunctioned," he says. The accident caused major damage to the vessel but no injuries to personnel. Barton's carrier spent three weeks in the Naples shipyards, then rejoined the fleet.

Continued on page 146

SHANE RICHTER
Sergeant E-5
US ARMY

Date of Service 1979 ~ 1985

SHANE RICHTER
Spokane, Washington

Touch football shouldn't lead to broken bones and bruises. But if you ask Shane Richter, he'll give a slightly different version of his pick-up games while stationed in Germany.

Richter had enlisted in 1979. "It gave me the chance to serve my country," he says. He had another reason for enlisting as well: the Army promised to help him earn the GED, and he jumped at the opportunity. Besides, several of his family members had served before him, including a grandfather in World War I and an uncle in Vietnam.

After training in field artillery, Richter was transferred to Frankfort, Germany, where he encountered a startling surprise almost immediately. "I'd just gotten there and met some of the men I would work with. I hadn't even unpacked my things when the alert horn went off at 5 p.m.," he recalls. He'd already heard about the random alerts, though he knew they usually occurred early in the morning. "I thought this was the real thing, but it turned out to be just another drill. The fact that I was so unprepared for all the things I needed to do for the alert really scared me."

But soon he learned the procedure and his part in the ensuing scramble. He also learned to use his free time judiciously—and traveled the country by rail. "I saw the Black Forest and Munich," he says. The lush German countryside delighted him. "My favorite place was a small town in the Black Forest where the train track ended. No one spoke English, and I learned a small amount of German."

During some of his free time, Richter and his friends played football. "There was a rule that it was only supposed to be touch football," he explains. But somehow the touch turned to tackle, and one or more of the guys would end up with an injury. So, how did they explain their rough play to the authorities? "When the game ended every week, we walked someone over to the dispensary because they broke a finger, an arm or got bruises. We always told the medic that it was only touch football and our guy fell down."

One of Richter's football friends became a close companion. "Joe and I served together in Germany and then at Fort Carson, Colorado," he says. "We were practically brothers, we were so close. We did everything together." One example of their antics involved New Year's Eve firecrackers. "We snuck a few fireworks into the base and lit them off and then ran like crazy and didn't get caught. Everyone wanted to know where the fireworks came from."

After Richter married, Joe stayed with him and his wife for a brief period. But when Joe left the service, he left the Richter home to find his own accommodations.

That's when things went bad.

"Joe got into a situation that was going to involve the law and probably some jail time," Richter recalls. "We hadn't talked for a few weeks. I knew there were some things going on with him, but I couldn't really

Continued on page 147

ROSE JOHNSON
Staff Sergeant E-6
US ARMY

Desert Storm

ROSE JOHNSON
Umatilla, Oregon

After her divorce, Rose Johnson didn't sit around and mope. She joined the Army and became boot camp's "old lady" at age 29. Unlike some of her younger counterparts, she breezed through the physical training, thanks to her civilian experience as an exercise instructor. And thanks to her family history, she had no trouble with relationships in the barracks. "As the oldest girl, but middle child of eleven children," she says, "I was used to being calm. I found that if I dealt with a problem after everyone calmed down, we would get together one-on-one or team up and solve the problem."

This skill came in handy throughout her years in the military. She believes her fellow soldiers often looked to her for encouragement. "That made me feel good about myself. They had faith in me when I gave them that positive influence," she notes.

While in the Army National Guard Field Artillery Unit in Missouri, she traveled across the country, "making sure all soldiers' records were up to date." During Operation Desert Storm, she volunteered for overseas stations, and she spent three months each in Panama, Germany and Italy. She handled her duties capably, thanks to her organizational skills. "In all the units I served in, I worked with records," she recalls. "Whether it was an MP unit, headquarters or medical unit, I always worked in records."

Johnson says the military allowed her to develop maturity and independence. "During my service, I learned that I could do anything I set my mind to. I could stand up on my own two feet. I didn't have to depend on anyone. I could do it myself."

Her most memorable moment came in Panama in 1995. "I was stationed in a hospital medical unit on the Canal," she says. "A group of soldiers was getting ready to go to the field, and we heard a bomb go off." Immediately, sirens and alarms blared, sending personnel scrambling in all directions. "I'd never been involved in anything like that before."

While Johnson and her unit remained unscathed, she would eventually see casualties during her military career—some close to home. "One soldier in my unit in Italy, named John, had a heart attack and died in the barracks," she remembers, noting the rarity of such an occurrence. More recently, one of her own brothers, Richard Davis, passed away in 2008. Another tragedy struck when her mother passed away. This occurred shortly after Johnson had transferred to the Oregon Unit. "Nobody there knew me," she says, "but my fellow soldiers comforted me, collected funds and helped me get to Chicago for her funeral services."

Thinking about the incident, she says, "I learned that serving my country was about people helping people. I got a lot of support when I needed it."

This "old lady" now works for the Union Pacific Railroad as a sheet metal mechanic repairing the locomotives. She chose that line of work rather than an easier secretarial position—once again proving she can do anything she sets her mind to.

APRIL BRESGAL
Tech Sergeant E-6
US AIR FORCE
WASHINGTON STATE NATIONAL GUARD

Desert Storm

APRIL BRESGAL
Spokane, Washington

April Bresgil says, "In 1974 I enlisted out of absolute desperation." She'd dropped out of high school several years earlier, and had spent the time since essentially homeless. However, recently things had settled down a bit. She had a place to live, had earned her GED, and had enrolled at Spokane Falls Community College.

Within a few weeks she discovered she was failing all her classes and withdrew. The problem, she realized was her home life was "chaotic," and she didn't know how to keep up with homework. "I had the brains," she asserts, "but I didn't have the stability or the discipline I needed. Walking down the street one day, I saw this recruiter's office, so I went in," she recalls. She met with a recruiter, enlisted in the Air Force, and for the first time in years felt hope. "I knew that if anybody could get me through school, they could."

While Basic Training had its difficult moments, Bresgal said she enjoyed it and the next four years of her first enlistment. The structure appealed to her. "In the service, somebody told me what to do. I did it. They patted me on the head, and I was a happy camper."

After Basic, she went on to Avionics Technical Training at Keesler AFB. "Basic Training and Tech School were both pretty easy. It was stressful because everything is new and because of the pressure. Pressure to keep your shirts ironed, bed made correctly, grades up and all of that – it was stressful, but not difficult."

She got good grades and moved on to her first assignment at Castle AFB in central California. She learned quickly, enjoyed her job, and was given several awards.

Even so, stress built up for her over time, rather than going down. The first on-going problem Bresgal encountered was with gender discrimination. "From the day I walked in the door for Basic Training, I dealt with sexism. Later, I was almost always the only female in our shop, and I usually had to teach the new guys how to treat me. 'No, don't try to carry my tool box. Yes, I can repair this transmitter, all by myself. No, I won't go out with you.'" So, in most cases, she says that problem went away over time. She says she worked with many 'wonderful men,' who were good friends and co-workers. "The best of them just treated me like any other member of the team. They expected me to pull my weight, helped me out when I needed it, and vice versa. Just like they would anyone else." However, there were many of the other kind of men, too.

Sexual discrimination continued, even after she "trained" all the guys she worked with directly. "Being treated differently from the guys was an on-going problem." There were always comments about "women drivers" when it was her turn to drive. There was always resistance to including her on exercises because of the "special" needs of women regarding privacy. And, finally, she says, "I feel confident that I didn't get promoted to Master Sergeant because my supervisors were afraid to deal with me in a supervisory role. They did not want to have to deal with me as a peer and didn't trust me to supervise the section."

Continued on page 147

SETH VAN EYCK
Staff Sergeant
US ARMY

Balkan War / Iraq

SETH VAN EYCK
Spokane, Washington

Born in Canada to American parents, Seth Van Eyck joined the Canadian Army at age 17. Shortly after infantry school, which he finished in 1992, he and other members of his unit got phone calls at 3 a.m. When he arrived on the base, he says, the older soldiers calmed his worries. "You know, this happens all the time," they told him. "We do these rapid deployment exercises, where we come in with all of our stuff, and they send us off for like half the day and then they send us home."

But this time would be different.

Van Eyck recalls, "We got on the bus and they took down our names. Then we drove out to the airport and started getting on the airplane. One old Corporal says, 'This has never happened before.' The next thing I knew, I was in Sarajevo, Bosnia, securing the airport so they could fly in aid for the people."

He finished that tour and stayed in the Canadian Army until age 23. But because he was so young when he enlisted, his body hadn't fully developed yet. "The growth plates were still shifting so my knees weren't working very well," he says. Besides, he had a few disciplinary problems due to his immaturity. As a result, he wasn't allowed to reenlist. "My intentions were to make a career out of the service, so that was a real disappointment to me."

But he had an alternate plan: the USMC. "I jumped in my pickup truck on a Friday and drove down to Montana with the express purpose of joining the Marines," he says. But a small inconvenience resulted in a new direction. "When I got to the recruitment office, on one side of the hallway was the Marine Corps, and on the other side was the Army. The Marine office was closed because they were at lunch. I turned around and went into the Army office and enlisted on the spot for six years as a tank crewman."

He joined in May of 1997, and by October he was in Korea. He also spent time in Bosnia and later in Iraq, where he served as a tank gunner with the 101st Infantry Division. His first combat experience occurred on New Year's Eve, 2005. Taking a Chinook helicopter to their base in southern Baghdad, he and others noticed an unusual sound. As Van Eyck tells it, "A kid sitting next to me said, 'Hey Sergeant, what's that tick, tick, tick I keep hearing?' I told him they were bullets." Indeed, people in Baghdad celebrated New Year's Eve by shooting into the air. Van Eyck still doesn't know whether the Iraqis were shooting directly at the helicopter, or if the chopper just happened to be flying through the gunfire.

In either case, he says, "Every male age 18 and older in Iraq had an AK-47. They were allowed to have it and one magazine of ammunition," which he describes as a rite of passage into manhood. Certainly, then, he wasn't surprised to hear bullets hitting the helicopter.

Continued on page 148

TOM I. DAVIS
Program Afloat
College Education
US NAVY

Date of Service 1978 ~ 1979

AFTERWORD
Tom I. Davis

Interviewing many people for VETS has been an eye opener. During all my years, I have never had a vet tell me their story. You might expect, in some bar sitting next to some person you'd never met or with a friend you've known forever, that they might open up and tell what's known as a war story. Never happened to me. Maybe vets tell vets war stories, but I doubt it. I think that the experience is sacred to vets, not to be blathered about. Interviewing the many veterans, whose portraits John has painted, has been valuable for me, has in fact, rounded out my understanding of America where ex-military hold sacred their duty, hold fast to what they know about living, about deep loss, fear and courage. These stories have rounded out my understanding, and I hold in awe these people. I look more carefully, now, at a passing stranger who, I know, knows more than I do about being an American. I was not a soldier and am humbled by that.

My experience of the Navy in the late 70's was a life saver. My life, having not been in the military, was not shaped by discipline nor limitation. My motto was "do what ever comes up." So by 45 I was ready for humiliation, limitation, escape from my marital blues. Ted Harper said "pray." I didn't know how. Pat Palmer said "Pray the Lord's Prayer." I did, a thousand times, at the stern of the Lois Anderson, a scow on the way to the Bering Sea, being there, going there, and coming home. Shortly after I finally got around to praying "help me, period," I was in Subic Bay awaiting the William H. Standley to teach for P A C E which provided sailors on board ship with the opportunity to earn college credit.

I was supposed to board the Standley in Hawaii, but it had been diverted to Korean waters because of some challenge there from North Korea. For the next six weeks I relaxed in the perfect weather of Subic Bay on the island of Luzon. I worked out in the gym and visited the Officer's Club. I took forays into Alongapo, a crowded city that serviced sailors' needs. Warned to not take a ride from a white jitney I did anyway and ended up somewhere in the interior of Alongapo where I was invited into a house by the polite and friendly jitney driver and was robbed by him and two other very friendly guys who poked me in the ribs until I took the 7 dollars out of my sock and handed it over. The entire scene was embarrassing for all of us. They, if anything, did not seem like the robber type though I must have seemed like an idiot.

When the fleet arrived in Subic Bay, the Coral Sea unloaded at least a thousand sailors onto the long dock; and I walked directly through these crowds directly up to my friend who had told me about this job in the first place. On board the William H. Standley heading for the Gulf of Oman, we had layovers in Singapore, where I got my modest tattoo. I traveled to the outskirts of the city to find a tattoo artist the sailors knew about. There were two Australian seamen there having tattoos completed that covered their backs. They were both drunk and puking so the artist and these blokes were slipping and sliding on a sea of vomit. In spite of this the tattooist was calm and friendly and well able to put a swallow on my left shoulder where it resides. My idea was that this swallow would bring me home, which it did.

We had a three day lay over in Bangkok, where I followed sailors around in the sweltering heat, so hot the sky looked black. We cruised to the Gulf of Oman where the Standley rode the calm green waters for six weeks beneath a communication satellite. One of the two massive engines blew a stack and had to repair to Diego Garcia for overhaul. Crossing the Equator I became a Shellback and remember not at all that I had to kiss the babies belly though I must have. I taught three English classes and was free on board in every space but the War Room because of my high civil service rating. My students were serious and mature. The Intro to Poetry class, that met in the forecastle and was attended by more than 20 sailors, without chairs or desks, reclining on whatever was stored there, was a pleasure to teach. One of my favorite students of all time was the Chief Petty Officer for the First Division, who was slow of speech, didn't read well, but was absolutely dedicated to learning; and his ability to share insight was inspirational. The Navy is a phenomenal enterprise that won my respect. With no exceptions in my experience on the William H. Standley, the morale among the crew was excellent. Duty performed with good will and enterprise made this period of time one of the most rewarding in my experience.

After returning home to Seattle, I was called to San Diego to board a ship whose name I've forgotten. It was one of a fleet of ships heading for the Western Pacific. After leaving shore side, I was as usual seasick for three or four days. My bunkmate was a young Philippino, an officer, who didn't understand why I was on board which was true of several of the officers in the Ward Room so I spent much of my time not in the Ward Room but with the enlisted men in their various spaces.

In my experience most of the guys who join the Navy are from the mid-west. Only one young guy in any of my workshops was from the west coast. I got to know him quite well, and he had decided he did not want to be on board. He started a protest out in the middle of the Pacific that led him eventually to jump overboard. One of the officers who hung out in the Ward Room was a Navy Seal who was being transported to his unit. The Navy Seal had taken a lot of hectoring so when the young guy from Deadwood, Oregon decided to protest by jumping overboard, the Navy Seal jumped in to rescue him to prove that he, himself, was indeed a hero. With my own eyes I watched all this come down. The troughs between the waves were at least 8 feet deep so, of course, the Seal couldn't see the sailor. Some of the ships in the fleet came into view for the first time while these guys floated around down below. The ship, along with the convoy, came to a halt and a life boat was sent over the side and the two guys were rescued. The guy from Oregon went to the brig and the Seal had to live with real humiliation for the rest of the trip hiding in his quarters.

We had a three-day lay over in Pusan, Korea which was still a fortified city with gun emplacements in the streets that were blacked out at night. Once I was strolling along a sidewalk not too far from the city center when a big guy coming toward me grabbed my arm, lifted it up, looked at the watch I had purchased from the ship store, scowled at how chintzy it was, and threw my arm down. He could have had it if he wanted it. My cruise on this ship was less than a month long. I don't remember teaching any workshops though I must have. I do remember that there was a library of several hundred novels and a gym where once and a while I lifted a weight. We stopped overnight in Japan then cruised to Okinawa from where I flew home.

My next adventure on board was on the USS Fletcher (993) at Ingalls Ship Yard, Pascagoula, Mississippi from San Diego. The cruise through the Panama Canal, where the skipper ran around and around the ship's deck to pay off a bet, was one of the highlights of this great trip. Calm seas, beautiful landfalls, 3 days in Cartagena, Columbia where I climbed up the wooded hill in the town and made friends with about 30 kids who were playing up there. While at sea I had some great English classes that made the trip itself good in every respect. Duty for the men aboard was not difficult so there was plenty of time for classes, but when we reached Pascagoula being on shore gave them liberty. I remember two young swabbies that I spent time with, reading many pages of A Pocket Book of Modern Verse; and they wrote some good poems.

I traveled with some of these guys to the Mardi Gras in New Orleans and to Florida. It was easy duty. It was good to be there because I was a William Faulkner fan, and Pascagoula was definitely his plot of ground. On the way to Pascagoula, I started with some good classes, but since we were shoreside on a giant ship's ways a sailor's free time was his own and classes lost attendance. With lots of free time, I developed great relationships with a couple young guys; and though I wasn't teaching classes, at least, I was helping them to pass the time and learn.

My experience aboard these great warships gave me an entirely different view of the American Military. There were serious jobs to be done on these warships and in almost every instance in my experience the men doing them were thoroughly trained and dedicated. Crews in all the different divisions worked well in teams and singly. I came away respecting the various ranks, responsibilities, and cooperation. These months aboard Navy Vessels gave me a new life. I returned home optimistic and full of zest. The balance and order on board helped to heal me of old wounds and made my life better. I believe this happens for many men on board ship who learn self-discipline and develop important skills. At 44 I gained that proverbial new lease on life aboard our proud Navy vessels, and I am forever grateful.

Tom Davis

I cannot.

I cannot remember the names of the men of my platoon who fought with me and died at the castle or the dozens of other villages and canals, ridge tops and mountain valleys. I only remember bringing back handfuls of dog tags.

I cannot stare down those battles in search of every emotional detail. I now realize the mistakes I made, the recklessness of my bravado, the myth of invincibility that only existed when I was young and naive--which is why we send the young and naive to fight our wars. If I put fifty-two years of knowledge and perspective next to the names and the memories of the men for whom I was responsible I court insanity.

After the first combat death splattered blood across my face I realized there is no glory. I numbed myself in order to go on. I divided my mind into compartments, putting emotion into one, soldiering into another. I lived and worked from the compartment of soldiering. If I made the mistake of getting too close to somebody, I forced myself to forget about it after his face exploded or his intestines spilled. I didn't dare sit and mourn. I had to keep my wits about me or I would end up being carried out on a stretcher or left for the vultures and blowflies.

Fatigue at first disarmed me--making me more vulnerable to grief. Soon fatigue was my friend, helping to deaden my brain and the part of my soul that wanted to well up, overflow, and drown me with grief. Occasionally I could not quell it and ended up heaving my guts out, first with bitter gushes and then racking, dry retches. It felt horrible, not so much for the stomach spasms or bile rushing out of my mouth as for the fact that I was losing control.

I never feared dying. I always feared losing control.

It's not that I don't love these men and mourn their passing. It's not that I don't count the ways I might have prevented their deaths. That's the luxury and the damnation of having the time and opportunity to look back. That's part of the haunting. But gunfire, mortar rounds, artillery shells, and booby traps don't allow any perspective. I focused on the desperate need to survive that moment, capture a few hundred feet of hillside, a trench, a machine gun nest. If I survived one minute, I figured out how to deal with the next.

After years of trying to forget, of regretting many deaths, I have been handed the hero's mantle. I wear it uneasily. People have considerable expectations of heroes. We are not to falter in the spotlight; we are not to have made many mistakes in the past. Being a black American raises the ante.

"Black youth so desperately need heroes such as yourself," well-wishers constantly tell me, as if this is the ultimate compliment. It is not. It is the ultimate pressure to constantly re-examine memories long buried in emotional self-defense. It magnifies my shortcomings and my guilt.

I did not seek this final chapter to my life. I moved to a remote cabin in the backwoods of Idaho, with easy access only to good elk hunting, to escape attention. The Army came looking for me as part of its own self-examination. Its historians created this heroic image, and the media happily made additions. The public added another measure.

Once handed mythical stature, I have not been allowed to step out of the spotlight. Even if the mantle fits me as sloppily as a father's shirt fits his infant son, I am expected to stroll about my stage as if my outfit was tailor-made. If I ask for something more my size, I will be cast as ungrateful. And with enough hype, media attention, time as a poster boy for this cause or that, I have magically grown into the shirt, this stature. At least in the eyes of the public.

I am not an icon for any ideal. I am an old soldier, a loner, a man more fit to fight wars than deal with peacetime society. My mistakes are as numerous as any man's. My regrets likely loom larger.

My hero's mantle has been crafted out of carnage, the senseless sacrifice of young men and my mad-dog desperation to outlast the enemy and disprove the fiction that black soldiers were afraid to fight. It is not cause for national celebration nor the incarnation of heroes. It is reason for us to mourn our losses and question our motivations.

I love those nineteen men like no other souls. I cannot give their names, but I carry their faces in my mind with nagging clarity. They visit me in the night, or when I'm sitting on a downed tree awaiting an elk. Or when some other small event triggers a memory of what we shared. The faces say nothing. They only stare at me with the final look they gave death.

These men, these faces, are the reason I am here today, the reason I was selected for the Medal of Honor. They are the heroes.

US Army Medal of Honor, Purple Heart, Bronze Star, Distinguished Service Cross

---

Archie Staley - Continued from page 5

Living in an olive orchard, they managed with minimal accommodations. Eight men—two full crews—shared a 14' X 14' tent, situated next to L-shaped trenches. Unfortunately, they had to endure one of the worst winters Europe had experienced in many years. Archie and his crew stayed warm in their tent by fashioning a heater from a five-gallon metal bucket with sand in the bottom.

As soon as Archie arrived in Lucera, he started an intense three months of bombing missions. The targets included key points of supply, such as oil refineries, rail lines, transport bridges and enemy troops. His navigator documented in detail all 51 missions in a notebook strapped to his knee during flights.

Archie describes his experiences in a factual, historical style. "We made the bomb run to Ploesti, Rumania, twice, and in between runs another group flew the Ploesti mission on the day called 'Black Sunday.'" Archie explains the meaning of the term: "On that day in 1944, Herman Goering sent a mass of German planes to Ploesti in an all-out effort to defend it."

To the Americans' dismay, Goering saved Ploesti, a strategic 20 miles of oil refineries, storage tanks, and structures, which provided one third of the German war machine's oil supply. Moreover, few of the Allied heavy bombers came back from that mission. Archie recalls, "The Germans shot down 54 of them. They fought against Goering's 'Yellow Nose' pilots, Germany's elite."

Archie and his crew did not have a flight on Black Sunday; he considered it luck.

Later, Archie experienced a different kind of close call. While on their way to Ploesti they took a direct hit on one of their four engines. The engine caught fire, and all the men left their positions, lining up to parachute out. But the thin oxygen at high altitude kept the fire from spreading. The crew waited four minutes as the flames died out. With grateful hearts they went back to their positions and returned to the landing strip on three engines.

Another mission proved to be even more frightening. Archie's crew was flying at about 15,000 feet when they received a barrage of FLAK from a train on a railroad. These deadly guns were ground-based anti-aircraft. The shells contained various fuses, which sent exploding shrapnel into the target area.

Archie noticed the damage behind his co-pilot's seat, and by the time they landed, the copilot had counted more than 35 holes. One 88mm shell had struck the plane from the bottom, hit eight inches behind the co-pilot's chair and exited through the top of the cockpit. As the plane slowed to a stop, Archie recalls, the co-pilot turned white. Without a word he picked up his chute and got on the truck that transported crews back to the camp.

Thanks to his years in the service, Archie received the Distinguished Flying Cross, the Air Medal with Two Oak Leaf Clusters, and the European African Middle Eastern Service Medal with Six Bronze Stars (one star for each Campaign). In October 1945, Archie boarded the USS West Point in Naples, Italy. He returned to Spokane by train and met Alene, and they finally enjoyed a short honeymoon at the Davenport Hotel.

Returning to the fields he loved as a child, Archie, along with Alene, raised wheat for the next 40 years. His contributions with fellow founding members of the Wheat Commission continue to benefit wheat growers today. Now, mending fences, building sheds and maintaining tractors keep him busy, and he helps neighbors by mowing their weeds and tilling their gardens.

He sat on the Spokane Armed Forces and Aerospace Museum board of directors for 18 years and currently assists their advisory board. Thus octogenarian Archie Staley, equally at home in a cockpit or on a tractor, continues to be of service.

This article was adapted from "Because He's a Wheatman,"
by Karen Allen, and used by permission of the author.

C. Bennett Crowley - Continued from page 9

C. Bennett Crowley - Continued from page 9

He married and became a father, but he would speak about the war only to his wife. Slowly, he learned to handle his nightmares and fears. His daughter recalls a family story typical of many whose experiences mirrored her father's. "My parents went to a baseball game together," she says. "When some airplanes flew overhead, Dad instantly grabbed Mother and threw her to the ground. He flung himself on top of her to protect her." Of course, the planes presented no threat, but his combat training surfaced nonetheless.

In his later years, C. Bennett Crowley opposed wars—up to and including the conflict in Iraq. Even so, he always asserted that if he could turn back the clock, he would still choose to enlist.

In a video of Crowley on his 90th birthday, his granddaughter asks him, "What's your favorite memory?"
He replies, "I don't have one."
Then she asks, "What is your least favorite memory?"

To this he replies, "Oh, I have tons of those!"

Moments later his great-grandson wonders in. After teasing him for a couple minutes, Crowley, with a big grin on his face, chuckles and tells the boy, "Don't worry kid, it's a good life—if you don't weaken."

That's good advice from a man who would know, seeing the horrors of war but being able to move past them.

Story by Judith Davis

World War II Victory Medal, American Theater Ribbon, Good Conduct Medal, European-African-Middle Eastern Theater Ribbon, Two Bronze Stars, United Nations Unit Citation

Frank R. Mace - Continued from page 11

On January 12, Mace and the others were transferred to Yokohama by ship. "The Japanese wanted to show their own people how most prisoners would be treated," Mace recalls, "so they beheaded five of the men right there on the deck of the Nita Maru. Then they just tossed the bodies overboard. Pictures were taken for propaganda, which later appeared in Shanghai and Tokyo newspapers."

And then it got even worse.

By January 20, the group of Americans moved to the Woo Sung concentration camp. Mace says, "It was very cold. Sometimes the temps were as low as 10 degrees." He and the others worked 16 to 18 hours a day, with little food. Adding to their misery, the captors beat them with bamboo poles drilled with ¼ inch holes. Mace describes the torture graphically. "When it hit our backs it would pop holes in the skin, so we had running sores most of the time. They never would get a chance to heal before we would get another beating. Since the only clothing we wore was a breech cloth, these beatings were extraordinarily cruel."

But somehow, in the midst of this horror, the enemy offered a snippet of mercy. In late 1942, Mace was made an honorary chaplain. He had the men build a kiln for the bodies of those who had died, to get the cremated remains of each person into a box, along with the man's name and personal possessions.

Another limited example of mercy occurred shortly afterwards. Mace suffered from a serious toothache, and the enemy allowed him to visit a dentist in Kobe. There he had four teeth extracted—unfortunately, without anesthesia.

Then he caught pneumonia, and his fever skyrocketed to 106 degrees. And, because of lack of food while a prisoner of war, the weakened Mace weighed only 107 pounds. He had been 187 pounds when he was captured.

The doctors didn't expect him to survive.

But he believes a supernatural occurrence caused a reverse in his condition. He says, "I don't know whether I was dreaming or having a vision, but there at the foot of my bed stood a figure with long hair, a white robe, and sandals on his feet. He reached out and took my hand. It felt like 220,000 volts of electricity was going through my body. He said, 'You have lots of work to do for me; get out of that bed and walk with me.'"

Obeying immediately, Mace says he got up and walked. The two of them went from one sick bed to another, taking each man's hand and sharing that jolt of electricity with everyone in the ward.

The next morning Mace's fever had cleared. He was soon released, along with the others in that ward. They later thanked him for his help, but Mace didn't take credit. "I always told them it was not my help alone but with God's help."

Back at the POW camp, Mace remained there until the end of World War II. His experience totaled approximately four years of beatings, near-starvation rations, inhumane working conditions, and numerous health issues, like beriberi, malaria, dysentery and hemorrhoids.

But the hellish conditions wouldn't last forever.

On August 18, 1945, Mace saw an American fighter plane fly low over the camp. He says the aircraft dropped a duffel bag into the center of the compound, filled with cigarettes, candy and news of the end of the war. Mace remembers the collective reaction. "All the men just put their arms around each other and cried like a bunch of kids."

Upon returning to the States after his ordeal, Mace got a pleasant greeting from his former employer, Morrison and Knutsen, in the form of a $1000 check. Even better, his parents met him at the train station and drove him to the family home. He still recalls that vivid memory. "Just as we pulled into the driveway, two horses came running into the yard. The two girls riding them greeted us. One was my niece, Marjorie Jamieson, and the other is the girl who became my wife, Marcia Lee Peterson."

Mace married and resumed his career as a carpenter. However, he couldn't manage the strenuous work, thanks to the lingering effects of malnutrition. He decided instead to study at Eastern Washington College, where he graduated in 1970. For the next 12 years he taught building construction in Alberta, Canada, retiring in 1982 and moving to Four Lakes, Washington. He once again became a chaplain and served for years at the VA Medical Center in Spokane. At age 79 he was honored with an award for 5982 volunteer hours. He now has over 15,000 volunteer hours.

When he compares his years as a POW to his current situation, he says, "I think that part of my life was hell, but now it is heaven." His military honors include the WWII Victory Medal, Asiatic-Pacific Campaign Medal, American Campaign Medal, a Purple Heart and P.O.W. 1500 hours.

To reflect his faith and to recall the memory of that life-changing night in the Kobe hospital, Frank Mace has written poetry, including the following:

> *Not a star was in the sky and clouds were gathering fast,*
> *When I gave my soul to Jesus to keep until the last.*
> *And this I know that He will do, for*
> *He will guide me wherever I go.*
> *So put your soul in the hands of Jesus, and*
> *He will lead the way out of the land of darkness*
> *Into the light of day, if you will only pray,*
> *If you will only pray.*

World War II Victory Medal, Asiatic-Pacific Campaign Medal, American Campaign Medal, Purple Heart, POW 1500 hours

David M. Garinger - Continued from page 13

"In addition, I was not the studious type. My drive was to build rather than study. As a minister you have to be a scholar and write sermons every week." So he found work as a builder.

Looking back, he has no regrets about his military service or his life afterwards. "I enjoyed my time in the military. I was overseas for 14 months and learned a great deal. Morale was good, and we stayed until it was over."

With a nod and a smile, he continues. "I've been blessed with a good and full life. We have four happy children, nine grandkids and ten great-grandkids. I've been a general contractor for 27 years and do architectural drafting. Recently I've been designing buildings for Riverview Bible Camp."

As a senior adult now, David has discovered a new talent—which has nothing to do with his skills on the shooting range 60 years earlier. "I'm a painter and have worked to become an artist, which is very satisfying. I've taken art classes and have done forty plus oil paintings since retirement. My wife has been loyal and supportive and has always encouraged me, and our love of God has given us strength to get through the hard times."

Good Conduct Medal, Asiatic-Pacific Service Medal

David Depue - Continued from page 17

"'Yeah, go ahead,' the Officer of the Deck said to me, so I did," David explains.

But when he returned to the *Atlanta*, he faced an angry officer: General Douglas McArthur himself. The general, standing on the quarter deck, spoke directly to the young seaman. "Did you have a good time using my car, son?"

The situation went from bad to worse. David says, "The Officer of the Deck called me over and told me to put myself on report. I said 'for what?' He said, 'for unauthorized use of a government vehicle.'

"'Well, I had permission,' I reminded him."

"He shook his head. 'Not for General Douglas McArthur's car, you didn't.'"

"I said, 'Oops' and did five days in the brig."

While crossing the Equator, David joined the Royal Order of the Shellbacks—and endured a good-natured initiation from those who'd experienced the trip previously. He also spent time in Australia and New Zealand, finally arriving in China on an operation called River Rat Patrol.

"We were military personnel that governed the river," he recalls. "That's all I'm at liberty to say. We were kicked out of China in July of '47 when China went communist."

Though he didn't see combat, he is considered a WWII vet, due to his service in the occupation forces after the war.

"I liked the military," Depue says. "If I hadn't gotten married, I would probably have been the oldest sailor in the Navy. I actually had 17-1/2 years in the military," in addition to his two under-age years in the Missouri Guard.

After he was discharged, he says, he adapted to civilian life. He had two sons, and both joined the Navy at age 17—just like their father. They even excelled in the boot-camp drills, also like David, who speaks proudly of their accomplishments.

But after his military service, David's sleep was occasionally disturbed. "I had this dream for years and years and years, where I was trying to find my ship. Then when I would find my ship, I couldn't go aboard because I didn't have a uniform and couldn't salute the colors."

One of David's sons served on the *Enterprise*, and David visited him aboard the ship. The experience became a turning point in his civilian life. "I met the captain," he recalls, "and he let me have a two-hour watch at the wheel. The captain said to me, 'You haven't forgotten a thing!' That was a great honor."

Even better was a surprising result afterwards: "I have never had that dream again."

David says he's enjoyed his faith and his life in the Navy. He recalls an example of the merging of the two: "When I was stationed at Alameda and living in Oakland, I went to a Bible school. On weekends we went down to the streets and picked up sailors and marines and other military personnel. We took them back to the church, called a port of call. I really enjoyed that."

David also likes writing poetry. At age 13 he wrote this for his mother:

> *To the dearest one on earth,*
> *the one who gave me my birth.*
> *The one who took me up on her knee*
> *and taught me things which ought not to be.*
> *One I would trade for no other,*
> *for she is my own dear mother.*

Combat Action Medal (4 Bronze Stars), Navy Gold Conduct Medal,
China Service Medal, Pacific Campaign Medal,
WWII Victory Medal, Navy Occupation Service,
Korean Service Medal (2 Silver Stars) Southwest Asia Service Medal,
Korean Defense Service Medal, Korean Presidential Unit citation,
Purple Heart, Navy Unit Commendation United Nations Service Medal

John Russell - Continued from page 21

"They got mad at me," he says, due to the transfer requests. "It was so scary. I had to ask for someone to be with me nights because some came in there and wanted medication. They were all over me with their syphilis and clap so bad, and I told them I couldn't give them any."

On one particular night, the patients' threats forced Russell to drastic action. "I took my 45 out and shot a hole through the ceiling. I said, 'Now get out of here and go to the hospital.' And they got out."

As he reflects on his military service and decisions made by the United States, he thinks about the bombs and their destruction. "Dropping the bomb was necessary to end the war," he asserts. "I wouldn't be here if it weren't for that. Our commanding officer said that we were lucky. We are all lucky."

After being discharged, John Russell married in Walla Walla, Washington. He and his wife both worked for the telephone company. They had four children, fifteen grandchildren, and one great-grandchild.

Asiatic Pacific Service Medal, WWII Victory Medal, Army of Occupation (Japan)

Ernest Fraijo - Continued from page 23

Back in the ship's kitchen, Fraijo did his best to take care of those who continued to battle in the days that followed. He still recalls a certain Marine gunner, who "was one heck of a Howitzer man. At 500 yards he could drop into a chimney."

The 50-year-old Marine would walk into the kitchen and ask Fraijo, "You got anything good to eat, Cookie?" In response, Fraijo gave him and his buddies whatever they wanted. As he recalls, "We would make ham sandwiches prior to the battles." They also prepared a "General Quarters Breakfast," consisting of steak and eggs. Fraijo remembers, "The guys would take steaks, make sandwiches with eggs, pop the yolk, salt and pepper them, and shove them into their shirts."

Fraijo and his ship traveled throughout the Pacific, stopping off near the Gilbert and Marshall Islands. Generally, they arrived after the battles, to search for downed ships to salvage. One of the most bizarre was a destroyer off mainland Japan. As he recalls, "It was heavy fog; you couldn't see anything, but we went into that fog and finally found that ship. It had been hit with kamikazes." The only bodies they located were those of two kamikaze pilots—but only the torsos. Incredibly, he says, one of them was a woman.

After his time on the *Gear*, he returned to Farragut. While on liberty, he enjoyed dancing the jitterbug to big-band music in the Spokane USO. "They had Artie Shaw there and Benny Goodman," he recalls. At one dance he noticed a young woman among a group. "She happened to be a little more attractive to me than the rest, so I went up and asked her to dance. She looked me up and down and said OK. We got to talking, and I asked for a date."

Within a month he'd proposed marriage and she agreed. "We went to a little Justice of the Peace named McCarthy. He was as old as I am now." Later, they reconfirmed their vows in a church ceremony.

The new bride worked as secretary to the commanding officer at Farragut, and Fraijo soon got orders for the USS *Sturgis* troop ship. But Mary Margaret didn't like the thought of her husband leaving. She approached the brass and asked why Ernest was being shipped out so soon after his last deployment. The commander, determining that Fraijo had been overseas almost three years, responded, "OK, we'll scratch him off."

So he was transferred to Seattle, with the rank of Baker Third Class. Why only Third? "I went up to as high as First Class but because I had such a hot temper, I got cut down because of fights," he admits. Still, he remained in active duty until 1950, serving on a variety of ships and in ports.

Did he make the right decision when leaving the military? He compares his starting salary to that of a comparable position in later years. "When I went in it was $27.50 per month, but recently a young recruit I know was knocking down $1400 a month."

With a laugh, Fraijo says, "I should have stayed in! I would have made a million!"

Otis Stutes - Continued from page 29

Some of his close calls occurred away from the war zone. While on temporary duty at Fort Lewis, Stutes was pinned between two 2-1/2-ton trucks. The resulting leg injury required a three-month hospital stay.

By this time, Stutes was married and had twins—a boy and a girl. After recovering from the injury, he transferred to assignments in Iceland and then Greenland, where he manned radar sites around the clock. His son easily recalls that duty. "The guys would play pool and drink coffee all night. I would go up with him because I was a little guy, and I would lay on one of the pool tables and sleep while he was up doing his shift." In addition, Stutes stayed busy with groundskeeping and running the snow plow around the Army post.

Near the end of his military career, Stutes had a life-changing encounter. According to his son, "He went into a Billy Graham Crusade and made a commitment to Christ." Shortly afterwards, in June 1968, he retired from the Army.

But he stayed connected to the military. For the next 17 years, he worked as an electrician in the Civil Service at Fairchild AFB. And he joined the NCO Club and the VFW. In the last years of his life, Otis Stutes told his son about some of his military experiences, but he never bragged. In fact, when Tom discovered his father's medals and commendations, including stars for five major battles, he said, "Wow, Dad, you're like a hero."

"No," he answered. "The guys who died are the heroes."

Still, the son begs to differ. He knows his father served admirably. "He loved his country, and that's the way he was raised and how he lived his life," he says.

Good Conduct Medal, Five Battle Stars, Purple Heart, Presidential Citation, Bronze Star

Neighbour himself was wounded by an 81mm mortar shell. "I got shot in my legs and my rear end and my fingers," he says. "I got a Purple Heart, and this hand was actually purple. My fingers were badly swollen."

But he still had a job to do. That very night a team of seven or eight Japanese slipped into their area and cut the Americans' telephone lines. In spite of his injuries—and a command from his lieutenant—Neighbour dashed for the trench to repair the wires.

Such an act put him in more danger. "Running along the road, I came upon two Japanese waiting for me. Blam!" But he survived, thanks to unexpected assistance. "When I came to, there were a couple Marines, and the guys that hit me, they were dead."

After his tour of duty, Neighbour says the military helped him complete his education. He earned a degree in clinical psychology and transitioned into civilian life. But he'll always remember the fateful decision he and his buddies made back in '42. Would the outcome have been different if they'd chosen another branch of the service?

He'll never know the answer to that.

IWO JIMA

Friends are but ships
That pass in the night
They go to the front
Then soon fade from sight

Life here is cheap
Death faces us all
One, now at your side
May be soon seen to fall

He smiles hello!
He is coming your way
But that shell was so close
Death saddens the day

The foxhole is wet
You must feel the sun!
You cautiously rise
That, you shouldn't have done

All seems, "self sufficient"
As deaths' red stream they ford
The most dubious sinner
Seeks prayer with the Lord

You're terribly weary
The battle grows hot
But you're almost oblivious
Then your best friend is shot

What more now is left?
A voice seems to say
Yet you carry on
Though that friend passed away

Now the conflict is over
All seems serene
Still you remember those days
And the things you have seen

Friends tell you to smile
The slate is now clean
They can't understand
They were not a Marine!

W.C. Neighbour…written March 8, 1945

recalls the importance of that new plane. "It could transfer the big boys, the Fat Boys, all over the world," he states. Explaining the nicknames of the bombs, he says, "Someone had come along with the name Fat Boy because it was fatter than the regular 500-pound bomb and consumed the whole bomb bay. We had to jack up the nose of a B29 that put the tail on the ground. We could only get it in the front bomb bay."

While handling one of these deadly bombs, Goldfoos experienced a heart-stopping moment of terror. Looking back, he says, "We were on the ground loading them into the plane. Of course, I was the person in charge of all of the loading. One of the fellows was controlling this elevator, a very large elevator, at the back of the plane. Somehow the cables got fouled up and the dolly that the Fat Boy was on rolled off the elevator. It was up about four feet in the air and the airplane just rocked and rolled because of the weight."

As the crew watched helplessly, the Fat Boy fell to the ground with a thud. "I closed my eyes and wondered if I was still there," William recalls. He admits, though, they all quickly realized the bomb wouldn't have exploded under those conditions. It hadn't yet been ignited.

As part of the mechanical crew, Goldfoos traveled extensively. He's thankful for those experiences. "We would fly into Japan, Taiwan, Europe, all over the world. There are very few places I have not been," he notes. "It's exciting to this day to think about it. I wouldn't want to take these experiences out of my life."

But much of his work involved top-secret activities. "The word was out about the 49th parallel, and there were rumblings going on up there. I had no idea what they were doing but I knew something was going on." In any case, Goldfoos' flights were kept under wraps, and he and his crew were not allowed to talk to anybody.

Goldfoos remembers one incident to illustrate the seriousness of this matter. Prior to a 1:00 a.m. flight from Castle, his crew decided not to go to bed. Instead, they went to town, and two of his men found a bar. "One of the fellows had a loose mouth," William recalls, even though the guy divulged only that they would be taking off at 1:00.

But when they returned to the base, the talkative member was arrested at the gate. "He was a good guy, but we were sworn that we would not have loose mouths. He was eventually sentenced to five years in Leavenworth."

After Goldfoos' discharge from the military, he enrolled in the Academy of Aeronautics at LaGuardia Field to become an engineer. For some reason, though, he never received the benefits of the GI Bill, so he had to drop out of the school. He returned to California and worked for North American Aviation on a fighter aircraft. "It was a good-paying job," he says, "and I really liked what I was doing. But unfortunately it was a government contract job that ended."

Afterwards, he became a self-employed farmer. He bought and operated the oldest olive grove in the United States for almost 40 years in Merced. Then he started a bicycle store, and he still manufactures a professional pedal called AeroLite, which he sells around the world.

Looking back on his life, he speaks with satisfaction. He did, indeed, play an important part in military history. But he doesn't take all the credit for himself. "I'm very fortunate," he admits. "In other words, God was on my side."

John Kozol - Continued from page 33

Corporation. We had a bunch of stores, and I was in charge of all their meat programs. That meat came out of a big plant down in California, and my job was to make sure all those stores got their supplies. It was a good job."

Eventually, John Kozol returned to Pennsylvania and married. But he heard about hunting and fishing opportunities in the Northwest, so he and his family moved. His grown children now live in Portland and Seattle—near enough for frequent visits.

But, says John, "I get along. I always have."

John lived to age 76 and died at home on September 27, 2009

Bobie Eby - Continued from page 35

Bobie Eby's strength today can't compare to his boxing stamina in boot camp, though he has no complaints. "A little short on oxygen," he says, "but it's coming back."

He continues life as he began it in 1932—enjoying simple pleasures and the land around him. He married, had four sons, and became widowed after fifty years of marriage. Each spring, he says, "I plant a garden near my home—tomatoes, cucumbers and squash." And his house, while still humble, is a vast improvement over the toilet-paper shack on the South Dakota countryside.

Korean Service Medal, United Nations Medal, Five Bronze Stars

---

Lloyd Humphrey - Continued from page 37

Still not enough? He dropped a couple of small rocks down the barrel, along with a few more leaves. But by now he envisioned a whole Russian battalion surrounding him, so he added several more pebbles.

Finally he felt secure.

He looked around again but didn't see any shadows moving. Leaving his post briefly, he shouted into the wilderness, "I've got a muzzle-loader now!"

With that announcement, he saw something move in the moonlight. Humphrey gave it a proper lead and touched off his muzzle-loader, firing from his shoulder.

After the blast—and when he'd recovered enough to stand up again—he heard the jeep rev its engine and drive away.

"Whoever it was, is gone," he thought, "and I'm probably in a world of hurt."

Hoping to hide evidence that his weapon had been fired, he dusted out the barrel with a stick and a piece of cloth torn from his shirt. Soon, the corporal of the guard came for him. Humphrey tried to explain what had happened, but the corporal didn't reply.

The next time Humphrey saw his training sergeant, the man sported countless bandages. And, when the captain heard of the incident, he said, "You like to shoot people so well, I'll send you where you can get a belly full of it!" With that, Humphrey finished basic training and transferred directly into combat in Japan. His first order of business in country was eight weeks of demolition training; then he joined a group of men with a variety of skills. Their activities included setting booby traps behind enemy lines, "prisoner snatching," and disarming or destroying enemy mines and ordinance which had landed but not exploded.

And then they went to Outpost Harry. There, the job remained similar to previous assignments—particularly to find and destroy booby traps. The area was calm when they arrived, but that wouldn't last.

Without warning, the Chinese attacked, wave after wave for 52 hours.

Humphrey, along with approximately 100 other soldiers at Outpost Harry, held off 7,000 enemy troops, killing 3,200 of them. Amazingly, many of the Chinese soldiers attacked without weapons, though some managed to grab a gun from a fallen comrade. The Americans had weapon shortages of their own. Some picked up c-ration cans, while others took off their helmets and battered the enemy with them.

On the third day of battle, Humphrey was wounded and evacuated.

The incident occurred moments after he'd congratulated himself on staying safe. As self-propelled 122mm rounds started coming in, he made a run for a nearby jeep. But his timing was off when he leaped toward the vehicle, and he landed short of his target. Fortunately, though, the jeep disintegrated from a direct hit, and Humphrey was only wounded.

Another soldier dragged him to the bunker, where Humphrey pulled himself to his feet, holding on to the tent pole with his left hand. That's when he realized his right side was paralyzed. Somehow he made it to the aid station, 150 feet away, and was loaded into an ambulance.

He recovered and continued to fight bravely in other skirmishes. All told, Lloyd Humphrey sustained four military-related injuries. The first, which was also the least serious, caused his mother the most concern. Even though he'd asked his superiors not to notify her, they sent a telegram anyway. She didn't even know he'd enlisted, much less that he was serving overseas. After all, he was only 16 years old at the time.

One can only hope she blamed it on the uncle, who'd signed him up for the military in the first place.

Story by Dick Bresgal

Silver Star

Martin Pegnam - Continued from page 39

After discharge, Martin attended Iona College in New Rochelle, New York. He graduated and went on to earn a master's degree at Boston College through the GI Bill. Next, he looked for a teaching job. While sitting in a hallway waiting for an interview, Pegnam struck up a conversation with another prospective employee, a woman named Nancy. An hour later, after both were hired, they went out together to celebrate. That began a relationship which later turned to romance.

Through the years of their marriage, Nancy notes, Martin enjoyed entrepreneurial adventures. They made weathervane jewelry, which they sold through Yankee Magazine. They ran Captain Jack's ice cream truck, with Martin's picture—in striped sailor's shirt, captain's hat and beard—painted on the side. They even tried photographing tourists in handmade Pilgrim costumes in front of a replica of the Mayflower. Nancy laughs as she admits; "Of course we always spent so much money on our ideas that we never made much of a profit!"

When Nancy looks back on her husband's life, she speaks fondly of his military career. She recalls lifelong friends he made in Italy and elsewhere, and she believes his experiences as a sailor were happy rather than strenuous. "Martin really did love those four years in the Navy. He had no great things to worry about. Somebody put food in front of him and gave him a bed and he really enjoyed those years."

Phillip A. Bren - Continued from page 41

up in the air. I saw the Russian officer in his conning tower run to his phone, so I immediately headed for Check Point Charlie."

Phil made the most of his free time in Germany with sightseeing and shopping. In a few instances his status as an American soldier smoothed his way. "I was in uniform, so I was free to go where I pleased," he remembers. One day he went into a liquor store, where a long line of people waited. "I could always go to the head of the line since I was in uniform. As I went in, the place just went quiet. This Russian officer was in line, and I stared at him while pretending to look at the bottles on the shelves. He began to turn red and was sweating. Then he gave me this glare like he was ready to kill me, and I winked at him and quietly walked out the door."

By contrast, Bren's on-duty time was filled with intense work. "We slept and ate in a quick-reaction alert area for seven-day tours. Our bombers sat in the QRA under guard. We were always waiting for the alarm horn to go off." When it did sound—night or day—Bren ran to open the safe and unlock the nuclear weapons. "The planes could be off in less than five minutes," he recalled of the British bombers. "When they rose up off the runway they would level off above the treetops and would never be seen until over their target."

Remembering the bravery and skill of his allies, and the joys as well as the dangers, Phil Bren recounts his military life with pleasure. "I spent 20 great years in the Air Force and retired as captain at Fairchild in 1978. I am totally enjoying the good life and am proud to be retired Air Force."

Tom McLaughlin - Continued from page 45

accident, but another friend just visited me recently," he says. "He and I were at Fort Lewis together and at Fairbanks. He came and visited last summer, and we spent a few days reminiscing. Another friend from Idaho has been out here twice to visit." Besides these, McLaughlin has other Army buddies who stay in contact by phone.

Such friends serve as a link to his days in the military—days his ringleader friend never had the opportunity to experience.

Ronald Decker - Continued from page 47

Perhaps, but beneficial nonetheless. Decker's years in the Reserves—especially during the summer camps—gave him the opportunity to meet good friends from a variety of socio-economic backgrounds. That experience helped to broaden his horizons in the lifetime that followed. It also has given him some knowledge of military affairs that helps his understanding of America's international policy issues.

Story by Kathleen Thamm

Ron Vietzke - Continued from page 49

Miraculously, they came to a smooth stop anyway. Vietzke says, "Afterwards, the pilot and copilot got us together and said nobody talks to anybody about this."

Following active duty, Vietzke served in the Reserves for eight years. He now appreciates the impact of the Navy in his life and encourages others to consider it. "I think every young person should do a year in the military. I think it gave me a little discipline."

But as he looks back at his earliest years—and the war bonds and gas rationing of his youth—he regrets his inability to understand the real issues of government, politics and the war itself. "I wish I had been more interested in history at that time," he says.

David Nordby - Continued from page 51

After his discharge in 1962, Nordby completed reserve officer candidate school. He'd come a long way since survival training. "But I didn't take my commission," he says, "because I'd have to sign up for five more years. I wasn't interested at the time." Though he regrets that decision now, he admits he had other things on his mind besides military. "Eight years of reserve and active duty were enough."

Allan Pratt - Continued from page 53

As sole librarian in this section, Pratt had busy periods but also considerable down time, which he used wisely. "There would be hours that nobody came to check anything out or turn it in. I must have read every book in the classified library. I got quite knowledgeable about what was going on around the world."

One day he got a surprising phone call—which had nothing whatsoever to do with libraries and books. It was the personnel director, who said, "PFC Pratt, I'm looking at your file here and I see that you have collegiate swimming experience. It looks like you were on the swimming team at Washington State College."

After a pause, the director continued. "I have something that might interest you. Our two swimming pools will be open from May 15th to October 15th. The Army unit here is required to provide two lifeguards, and the Air Force is required to provide two, and the Navy guys are required to provide two, so that's six guards. The University of New Mexico will provide the other six guards for the summer."

Pratt quickly saw where this was leading.

"I'm offering you a job if you would like to have it," the director concluded.

Looking back, Pratt says he responded with a question. "How much time do I have to think about this?" With six months left on his tour of duty, he wanted to be sure the job timed out correctly.

The director replied, "I'll give you ten seconds, you SOB!"

So Pratt took the job and removed himself from the library's "big safe."

Lifeguarding suited him well, and he remembers only one close call. "It was when the Air Force Lifeguard got drunk and passed out and hit his head on the side of the pool and went to the bottom. That was the only rescue I made the whole summer."

He liked the job's benefits. First, his uniform was simple: swim trunks. Second, he ate well. "They released us from the mess hall and gave us passes to get in the hospital mess where the doctors and nurses ate. They said we needed better food because the hot desert sun in New Mexico was sapping our energy. That's how I finished my time there."

A third benefit came in the form of another lifeguard. One of the six from the University of New Mexico, he says, was "a gal by the name of Carol Allen, who was a cheerleader at UNM. She later became my wife."

Pratt completed his two years in the Army. "I never got past PFC and knew that I wasn't going to," he states. "When it came time for the exit interview for star performers, who got leaned on to stay in the service, I didn't experience that aspect in the interview. We had a mutual understanding. I was happy to be going, and they were happy that I was leaving."

Robert Lee - Continued from page 55

Another aspect of Lee's accounting job involved monitoring payments to Korean companies who were contracting with the U.S. Army or the United Nations. "There seemed to be quite a bit of money going out to the local economy," he says.

But Lee didn't simply sit at a desk punching an adding machine. He needed another skill set, in case North Korea decided to invade. His secondary training involved driving two half-ton trucks for evacuations.

Lee's tour of duty totaled 21 months and 13 days, which gave him less than 90 days to complete his military obligation once he returned to the States. His wife joined him in San Francisco, and they considered settling there permanently. However, California didn't feel right to them, so they moved to Portland, where Lee took a job with the same accounting firm he'd left when drafted.

In Portland, he joined the Reserves and was assigned to the 104th Transportation Reserve Unit as company clerk. Later, he was reassigned to the Army Administrative Center in St. Louis, Missouri, due to his specialty.

While casual observers may not equate accountants with combat soldiers, Robert Lee has proved them wrong. Although this college grad started as a private, he eventually gained rank. "Somehow I was promoted to an E-4," he says with a smile. "How I got it or when I got it is still a mystery to me."

Norman Wiegele - Continued from page 57

Clarence, continued to write, but Wiegele eventually lost contact. "I mean," he says, "in a way I wish we would have been closer."

Even so, he's thankful for his time in the Army—for both the truck-driving and the clerking. Afterwards, he worked a variety of jobs, and in each case his military experience proved beneficial. "I had people skills," he says. "I wasn't outspoken, but I tried to resolve problems. And, of course, people in the workforce are by far more challenging than people in the military service."

William Overholser - Continued from page 61

of their flight suits, crew chiefs and door gunners would get their aircraft tidied up and then a good number of them would go out to party. As our quarters were in villas in the town it was a walk across the street to see the bar action, then go to bed, get up the next morning, and truck out to this makeshift steel-planked airfield where the choppers were parked and go off and fight the war again." He says a gruesome day job coupled with a fun evening didn't suit him. The married men he knew didn't participate in the night life. "It just wasn't good at all," he states.

By contrast, when his unit moved to Bien Hoa, they got into the 24-hour-a-day routine of war. That's because "the Long Toms shot right over our tents all night long. Then the Air Force maintenance teams taxied the F100s, 101s and 105s to the exhaust barriers, which pointed right to where our tents were, cranked them up, and tested the afterburners." Such noises of war reminded them constantly of their mission.

Among their most important helicopter transports, Overholser says, were the injured. "I did a lot of med-evac flying—picking up and bringing back the wounded and dead paratroopers of the 173rd. Sometimes a medic would accompany us, but not always. The 173rd had to keep the medics with the engaged troops. We just got them out of there as quick as possible." In addition, Overholser's chopper carried rations, ammo and other gear. He said the cargo varied from chain saws and gasoline to ice cream and grenades.

Because Overholser's original plan didn't include a military career, he felt ready to resume life as a civilian after his 12-month stint in Vietnam. He hoped to get a job as a commercial pilot, but the military had a surprise for him. "I was informed that I was not going to be released and because I had accepted the regular Army commission rather than the Reserve commission I served at the pleasure of the President of the United States. I was a captain, and if I was going to stay, I would go to the Infantry Officers Advanced Course." The one drawback was another two- or three-year obligation, but he liked that idea better than returning to Vietnam. Besides, he says, "I was satisfied we were winning and it would soon be over."

On completion of the yearlong course with the war still dragging on, he volunteered for a second tour in Vietnam and the Cobra Attack Helicopter course to get it over with and get back to pursuing a career in the airlines.

As a Major he was assigned to another assault helicopter company, the 240th AHC, as the Commanding Officer. By now the Viet Cong had shifted to small-unit tactics, and his mission became almost exclusively search-and-destroy. "On a typical day there could be as many as 10 to15 insertions and extractions. Sometimes we would split the company up into two flights of five, and we would put five loads of GIs in one area and five loads in a totally different location. Sometimes they found the enemy. Sometimes they didn't. If they did, we had to reinforce them, usually under fire; and it could get complicated dealing with the wounded, combat damage to the helicopters, rearming and refueling."

When Overholser returned to the States in 1969, he couldn't help noticing changed political attitudes and war resisters. "Jane Fonda had some splendid thoughts," he says sarcastically. "I still get e-mails from old Army friends that pass on the Jane Fonda betrayal video."

Like many of his contemporaries, he avoided the topic back then. "I never mentioned Vietnam for 20 years—'69 to '89," he says, shaking his head. "What am I going to say at a dinner party? 'Oh, by the way, I don't know if you know this; but I'm a Vietnam vet. You want to hear about it?'"

Even so, he didn't forget. He read several books on the Vietnam War to try to make sense of it and the impact on America. Among his favorites were *Chicken Hawk*, *Bright and Shiny Lie*, and *About Face*. He studied the historical causes of the Vietnam conflict and came to a conclusion: "It boils down to what the people who were running our government thought was the best thing to do. They thought the best thing was to stop these smaller countries from falling into communism which was known as the "Domino Theory."

He understands opposing perspectives of the conflict. From one viewpoint, he says, "It was a horrible mistake, too costly in lives and certainly caused internal social unrest in America." The other way to look at it focuses on what it accomplished. "Did it do any good?" he asks, then replies to his own question. "Frankly, I don't know the answer to that."

In 1974, Overholser was assigned to Argentina as a foreign area specialist. He had completed a Masters Degree in political science and history, and both he and Marilyn studied Spanish for six months.

There as in Vietnam, he, and now his family were in the midst of terrorist activity and war-time horrors— "where a guy walks out his front door and gets mowed down by terrorists, which happened almost on a weekly basis. Some Argentine military person, usually in the rank of major or above, was the target of the assassins." He believes the terrorists targeted ranking people, "to show that the government couldn't protect its own people and to prove the government couldn't stop the terrorists." This became known as the Argentine "Dirty War" and there are protest marches to this day in downtown Buenos Aires.

In 1976, Overholser returned to the States and for two years assumed command of the ROTC Program at Washington State University. At WSU, in response to the campus antiwar movement, the ROTC instructors had at some point begun to wear civilian clothes to work and change into military uniform once in their offices. Overholser, now a Lieutenant Colonel, began to wear his uniform to and from work and soon all his officers and NCOs were doing the same. The previous year, he recalls, "They had demonstrations in the stadium, kids throwing red meat onto the track, and all that sort of thing—demonstrations against Vietnam."

Overholser's last two years in the military were as the commander of the University of Idaho Army ROTC program. His service had come full cycle from his start as a cadet at Idaho and now as the commander.

Ever since his college days, Overholser's plans had to be adjusted numerous times, thanks to the Army. But all that eventually changed. "When I had served the military for 20 years, I made the decision to resign and got out."

Finally he could plan for life as a civilian.

Silver Star, 3 Distinguished Flying Crosses, 2 Bronze Stars with V Device for Valor, The Soldier's medal Meritorious Service Medal, 2 Army Commendation Medals including one V Device, Vietnamese Cross of Gallantry LTC Bill Overholser flew 1820 combat hours in helicopters in the Republic of Vietnam in two tours, 1965-1966 and 1968-1969

Robert Mecham - Continued from page 63

And, memories from his own dental practice at Lawton can still stir emotions. For example, he recalls a young officer from West Point, on his way to Vietnam. "I'd done a lot of work on him," Mecham says. "He was a super-sharp individual, like the West Pointers are. I always remember doing all that work and then, hearing by word of mouth a couple of months later that he was killed in action."

In 1973, Mecham faced the same decision that many would-be career military personnel face. Should he re-enlist? He considered carefully, because as a Reservist, he wouldn't have to dedicate himself full-time to the military. In addition, he was offered the job of interviewing congressional appointees to West Point, which he would've enjoyed.

However, by now he had four sons. And, with a full-time civilian dental practice, he didn't think he could handle the busy schedule. Though he believes he made the right decision to leave the military, he says, "I have wondered if I should have done that. It would have been an interesting thing, but once again, time was limited."

Benjamin White - Continued from page 65

remembers. The men were not allowed to wear uniforms or carry identification. The MIC (Man in Charge) was the one with the most expertise in that phase of the mission.

During his time in Southeast Asia, White often endured brutal conditions. But the worst was the long-term incident with the broken back. His rescue eventually came—from a surprising source. "I got out of there when two fishermen found me."

He remembers that Lieutenant Colonel Black had spread an announcement to local villages, to prevent the mutilization of Americans' bodies. The colonel offered $200 for "any cadaver returned to camp." Of course, when the fishermen approached White, he didn't know if they would kill him and return his body for the reward. He couldn't speak their language, and they didn't know English. But for reasons he'll never understand, they took him back to camp without further harm.

White suffered other injuries during his tour, including numerous broken bones and bullet wounds. But he wasn't alone. "Nobody came back uninjured," he says. In fact, only seven of them came back at all.

Years later White still feels the effects of battle. "I have metal in my head, metal in my chest, some metal in my spine and metal in my knee." In addition, he's endured skin cancer, psoriasis and PTSD.

To illustrate the extent of his trauma, he remembers the Christmas of 2001, when he gave his wife a kitchen faucet. "The pain I was having from trying to install it was so great. I was lying on my belly and my legs were twisted around." Three hours later he went to the hospital handcuffed to a gurney. "My wife was trying to soothe me and I didn't know who she was," he says, explaining that he sometimes loses sight of reality. "That's why I wear a rubber band on my wrist. I can snap it to bring me back to the here and now instead of there and then. I've raised a blister on my wrist, snapping it for as long as 35 minutes."

After the military, White moved from El Toro, California, to northern Idaho, where he has worked a variety of jobs, including construction. He worries about the direction the United States is taking, particularly concerning his right to bear arms. Above all, he recalls his days in Southeast Asia. "Why were there only seven of us that came back? We all received the same training, from the same people." Because his question cannot be answered, he may never experience complete peace of mind.

"I have survivor guilt," he says. As a service to his fellow veterans, White is presently the Assistant Chaplain in the Priest River, Idaho Chapter of the Disabled American Veterans.

Virgil Joe - Continued from page 67

commanding officer pulled it back and asked what time they were feeding. Joe's no-nonsense reply assured the commander that the curtain would be raised when the meal was ready—and not a moment before. "When it's up, it's time. Sir!" he barked to the superior.

In response, the CO said, "OK chief," and backed off.

Joe remembers the situation and admits, "I was the only cook that really took charge and made decisions, and that's why I got away with a lot."

When Joe arrived in Vietnam, he suffered from the heat. But the following winter brought another kind of problem. "Monsoon season was cold and lasted three months," he says. "The tanks would tear up the roads. We had to use the crapper just across the road. It sounds easy but it isn't, because you're in mud up to here." He gestures toward his knees. "So you drag one foot out, put it forward, drag the other foot out. Ten minutes to get across the road. You never stay dry or warm."

Returning to the States after eleven months, 22 days and 18 hours, Virgil Joe says his only "injuries" were PTSD (post-traumatic stress disorder), shell shock and battle fatigue. Making matters worse, he says, "We had to fight that war and then come home and fight the peaceniks. I'm a Native American and my heart ached."

Still, he carried on, enrolling in the Chef Program at Seattle Central. But his military past occasionally surfaced. "Once I beat the crap out of this guy near Seattle Central," he remembers. The man had called him a baby killer, and Joe's anger kicked into gear. "Whap, whop, he's down," Joe says, remembering his response.

When a police officer arrived on the scene, Joe offered no excuses. "I said, 'Look, I did it to him.' The cop says, 'What unit?' I say, '630 Combat Engineers 45th Group.'"

With that, the officer nodded. "I'm a bro, too." He named his own unit, then cautioned Joe, "It's tough, but you can't keep doing this."

Over the years, Joe has regained his stability, but he wants civilians—as well as mental health professionals—to understand the trauma. "I tell people, don't startle me. Don't walk up on me while I'm sleeping, because you don't know where I'm at. I may be in a dream state, a nightmare. There's good and bad days. Sometimes I'm OK and other times I'm not."

Musing on his year in military conflict, Joe says, "A Vietnam vet never comes home completely; he will always be there." He notes that of the 52 personnel who traveled with him to 'Nam, only two came back. "It was tough—big-time tough—because I went through basic with some of these guys."

Two weeks after he returned home, he received a distressing letter from his sergeant. "It said that half the team was over-run," Joe states. "Half the company!" Such news devastates even the strongest of soldiers.

Joe remembers his response: "I dropped the letter, went across and got two cases of beer, went up on the butte and cried."

Dennis Burgi - Continued from page 69

As in any unit, Dennis and his buddies worked under a variety of leadership styles. "We had two officers that were opposite ends of the spectrum," he recalls. "We had a guy we called Squeaky 'cause he squeaked about everything." A stickler for military protocol, this officer reminded Burgi of his boot-camp NCO. By contrast, Burgi remembers another lieutenant nicknamed Boogaloo, "because he was always boogieing around, and he had a great sense of humor. He always made you feel part of the team. It wasn't officers in that helicopter; it was men together. We were very close to Boogaloo. If we went through a hard conflict, when we hit port next time he'd go buy us drinks."

To highlight the difference between Squeaky and Boogaloo, Dennis remembers an evening at an officers' club. "One night the enlisted guys stormed the place. Squeaky tried to write down names to write us up, but Boogaloo was hollering, 'Go for it! Have a good time!'"

Of course, the good times were overshadowed by the frequent dangers while on duty. The crew faced grave concern when an aircraft came back too damaged for a safe landing. Burgi recalls one such sobering incident, when the arresting cable broke as the plane landed. "It killed a guy that was out on the deck at the time, cut him in half," he says. "The pilot couldn't stop." However, the plane's slow speed wouldn't allow the pilot another take-off, "so he went over the front end, and the ship ran over him. We never even saw any part of him or the airplane."

On another occasion, a torrential rainstorm caused serious problems. Burgi recalls, "The water was coming over the bow," which amazed the crew because of the 90-foot distance from flight deck down to the water's surface. "They wanted us to get ready for the launch the next day, and I told them, 'Can we wait? It's so slippery out there on that tar with the water.'" But the officers insisted. Burgi, inside a helicopter on deck, operated the brakes, while the crew pushed the chopper toward its parking place near the edge. "Just then, the entire ship tipped way over so the chopper's picking up speed. I hit the brakes and it didn't even slow down. I just jumped out."

Even with nets around the edge of the flight deck, the helicopter continued sliding. "It went over, and the wheels hit in the net, tipping it right over. Never saw that one again," Dennis says. "We lost a million-dollar helicopter—but no lives."

Men aboard the Kittyhawk generally avoided political talk, even though their families back home found it a common topic. Burgi and his friends recognized the differences between World War II and later conflicts—both politically and militarily. "At least in WWII you had uniforms," he notes, "and you could tell the enemy. Not in Vietnam and the same thing in Iraq. You don't know who the enemy is. We never talked about it. The politics of it never came up, because there were too many guys that would be deep into combat and other guys who like me wanted basically nothing to do with it. The thing was that often these were your best buddies. You don't need to get in an argument with them over something like that, that you can't change."

Another touchy subject involved race. Burgi remembers a fellow soldier—the only black man in his unit. Within their group they were close friends, but they discovered problems in other settings. Dennis explains: "When we had liberty in the Philippines, we hit a town. They had a black section they called The Jungle, and they had a northern section where everybody else went. If you were white, you didn't go down into The Jungle, and if you were black, you didn't go out of The Jungle. We wanted to go drinking with him, so we took him with us one night, and he got insulted by a few guys. A big bar fight broke out, and we felt satisfied when it was over that they weren't going to say that again."

Later, the black buddy took Dennis to The Jungle. "He was a big guy," Dennis says, "so I wasn't going to worry about it." Unfortunately, Dennis soon found himself in an uncomfortable situation—when his friend went to the restroom. "They started talking a lot of crap to me, shoving me around. The next thing you know, he comes out of the bathroom, and there was a big fight. We got tossed out. So we went back to the bar in the white section, where we'd already solved that issue and had no problem."

Dennis Burgi completed his four-year enlistment more quickly than expected. He says, "I was in three months shy of four years, because they had what they called three-month early-outs at that time. They would let you out three months early for some reason or another. I wasn't going to complain."

But like many Vietnam vets, he holds unhappy memories of his return to the States. He couldn't understand the attitudes of civilians toward the military. "I was bitter about a lot of my experiences when I got back. People would ask and I wouldn't tell them I was in the service, because every time it would start a fight. So I didn't talk about it." Comparing his homecoming to that of veterans of the previous generation, he says, "A guy in WWII would come back and be treated like a hero. They were proud of him, but Vietnam vets never saw that."

Today, he considers younger vets. "When I saw people going off to Iraq, I thought 'Oh, God, I hope they aren't treated like we were.'" But he's happy to observe civilians' more positive attitudes now. He takes pleasure in the small and large gestures of thanks and respect given to current soldiers.

After being discharged, Dennis worked at the Fresno airport, repairing aviation radios and radar equipment. Later he found work in the concrete industry and with the Forest Service. But he felt restless and decided to travel. "I had seen a lot of the world, but I had never seen the US. I was hitchhiking, thumbing it. I had a few scary moments, but I went all the way back to New York and across through Minnesota, parked cars on the ferry on Lake Michigan to get some extra money and came back through the southern states, Texas, Louisiana."

Now, in his later years, he deals with health issues. Some, he says, are results of medications. "I just had this really bad pain, and I couldn't even move my hand; I couldn't open a door. A couple of times I called the VA and said I'm having a lot of aches and pains from this medication. They said it will go away." But the pain persisted and worsened.

Burgi persisted, too, and he eventually found someone who listened to his complaints. In response, a newer staff member at the hospital proposed a blood test that measured pain level. With a "normal" reading of 11 or 12, Burgi's was off the chart at 81. The medic told him he could have died.

Relieved, Dennis says, "They finally ended up changing my medications. I still have pain in my wrists and my knees, but pretty much everything else is so much better."

That's definitely good news for a guy who prefers saving to killing any day.

Vietnam Service Medal, Bronze Star, Korea Expeditionary Medal

---

Ben Cabildo - Continued from page 71

Ben Cabildo - Continued from page 71

painted a picture of the demonstrators as weird, not Americans but anti-Americans. We continued to do our jobs, but we questioned a lot within our ranks, as well. Why were we there?"

As they pondered such questions, they looked beyond themselves to consider their training about the Vietnamese. "We were taught that they were not really people that we were fighting. They were Gooks. We didn't mind just shooting them because they were less than human. We did what we were trained to do, but we started questioning things."

He notes that morale was low as a result. In addition, soldiers feared unpopularity among the South Vietnamese. "We'd go out during our free time, and they weren't friendly," he recalls. "They would say to me, 'What are you doing here? You look like one of us.' I'd say, 'I look like a Vietnamese, but I'm an American.'"

A further problem involved the soldiers' attitudes toward officers. Cabildo says, "There was discrimination on that level as well. We started to be aware of a lot of injustice and unfairness within our ranks." He recalls a few reports of rebellions and fights in other companies against new, inexperienced lieutenants. And, he believes military authorities were discriminatory, particularly with promotions. "There were many soldiers of color who were singled out and court marshaled," he says. "They were treated as scapegoats. All these things disillusioned me with the military."

Still, he performed his duties and did his best to keep peace within the ranks. He was transferred to Vung Tau, where he finished his tour. In spite of nightly volleys of incoming rockets, he had little fear—until his enlistment was almost completed. "It became very scary when I had only 30 days to go before I left Vietnam," he admits. "That was the scary month." He had a few close calls but came back to the States without an injury. Ben served two tours in Vietnam and received two Army Commendation Medals.

Memories haunted him afterwards. "The first year I returned from Vietnam, if I heard a motorcycle or a car backfiring, I'd hit the ground," he says. "Also, it's hard for me to see a war movie, especially a Vietnam War movie, because it saddens me so much that I start crying. My heart is very heavy because of those experiences."

Cabildo does not romanticize his Vietnam tour nor the Americans' presence there. "It is not the right thing to be in somebody's land. That's what happened. It saddens my heart. War is not a necessary or essential part of living. War is created to control or to make a profit, because there is no real reason to make war."

He goes on, "If I knew what I know now, I wouldn't have gone to Vietnam. We were so young. We were self-centered. We were partying. Then we were put in a situation where we killed, or we would be killed. That's harsh. You can call it brainwashing, dehumanization. We wouldn't have been able to carry out the work we did without being dehumanized. We just didn't understand why there had to be war."

In spite of his attitude toward combat, Ben Cabildo concludes on a positive note. "What I really learned from Vietnam," he says, "was about understanding people. People have such talent. I can see them blossom at their untapped potential. That's what I love doing. I understand who they are and what they can become. I really treasure life."

Ralph DeCristoforo - Continued from page 73

person actually died on the battlefield," he asserts. "We saw guys coming out of Korea that had been killed up in the DMZ that we weren't telling our country about." Other unofficial deaths, he notes, included military personnel who did not carry IDs because of their highly sensitive work.

DeCristoforo completed his tour and returned to the States, remaining in the Air Force for 24 years. Like other vets of his generation, he muses about the anti-war sentiment that greeted him upon his return. While he and his friends didn't like the war's morphing into a "media event," they had no real quarrel with the protestors. "We didn't want to stop anti-war demonstrations, because this is America," he says. He echoes the sentiment of many retired military personnel who say, "America isn't perfect, but if I'm gonna be somewhere, is there someplace other than this country where I would rather be?" Their common answer was "no."

Occasionally he considers—then dismisses—the possibility of a do-over. "I don't have any regrets. Would I have done it the same way again? When I look at what the potential was in the neighborhood back on the block, I probably would."

Douglass Livingstone - Continued from page 75

your assess off." When Livingstone heard that, he refused to stay for the remainder of the speech. "I walked off toward the chow hall to have lunch," he says.

That same lieutenant took the platoon on a sweep the next morning and suffered heat stroke. Livingstone went up the column to see why they had stopped. The new lieutenant was lying on his back. Livingstone asked the medic, "Is this the guy who was going to hump our asses off?" Livingstone encouraged the medic to dust him off because they were out of water, and if he didn't he'd have twenty-five more guys just like him. Sure enough, the lieutenant fainted 100 yards later and the medic was convinced.

"I should have kept a diary," Livingstone now admits, trying to remember more of his combat experiences. Yet, when he returned to the States, he wanted to forget it all. He recalls arriving at the Seattle airport. "When we got to Sea-Tac, I went in the men's room and threw everything in the garbage and put on civilian clothes.

That was it. I was done." Unfortunately, he and his buddy Tracy lost sight of each other, "because I just wandered off," he states. It would be forty years before they would meet again.

Trying to adapt to life without war, he says, challenged him to the core. "I was so messed up, I couldn't focus. I was in a daze for a long time. All I could do, you know, was work my way out of it."

He stayed busy and hid from his memories, but nothing seemed to revive him. "I can't explain it," he says. "There were experiences that would kill me today, would drive me un-fit. I turned into a recluse."

Douglas Livingstone says he hasn't changed much since the Vietnam conflict. Sometimes he wakes up in the night, screaming. Though he doesn't have a vivid picture of his disturbing dreams, he tries to push them out of his mind. "Usually," he muses, "you want to know what you dreamt, but not these. I don't want to have anything to do with what it was that woke me up."

Thomas Poff - Continued from page 77

But he recalls one specific mission when everything went bad.

"I was making sure it wasn't an ambush. I jumped and got about 20 feet from the door," he remembers. "Something didn't feel right." But before he could yell "bush" to indicate an enemy ambush, he was hit. "When I got hit, the guy behind me also got hit and pulled the trigger of his 12-gauge. I caught the 12 gauge and the sniper round—double wammy."

Amazingly, he survived both. "The doctors called it my refusal to die," he declares. But the recovery wasn't easy. "I came out of the Naval Hospital after four months in a coma, with bullets in the back of my head. A scar runs for seven inches at the back of my skull."

Not everyone fared as well. "There were 116 men in my unit called The Devil Dogs, and 12 of us came back," Poff says. And now, he's the last one still living. Emotions almost overcome him when he remembers his comrades. "Friends I would die for, people who would stand behind me and take bullets to make sure I didn't. How many people are you going to find like that on the street? Or in life?"

Poff appreciates the military and the work they're doing now in the Middle East. "I have more respect for the people over there in that desert and in Afghanistan," he states. "I hurt when I hear one of them has died. It just tears a piece of me out because I know what it's like to lose a man in combat."

As he sits in his living room, the one-time "wild child" holds his head high. He points to his clock with its Marine Corps logo, and to his USMC cap with its sniper pin. "There will never be a day you will hear me say I am an ex-Marine. There are no ex-Marines," he declares. "There may be ex-Army, ex- Navy and ex-Air Force, but a Marine is always a Marine. Semper Fidelis!"

After a pause, Poff adds a final thought. "I have one poem that I want to put in your book. This is one that will make everybody, not veterans alone, think. *Man spends so much of his life killing time, but in reality, it's time that is killing man.*"

Joe Richart - Continued from page 79

"Between the Veterans Hospital in Spokane and in Seattle, I have received wonderful help," he states. "I couldn't ask for any better. I went to the Seven-West Clinic in Seattle for treatment for my PTSD. The first time I went, I had the idea that there was no way I needed to see a shrink. It took some digging, opening up the old wounds to let out some of that pain."

Now an outpatient at the Spokane Veterans Medical Center, Joe continues to have his medication monitored. He has learned to cope with PTSD and live a normal, productive life.

Still, the memories remain. "There were only six of us left alive out of 52 that we started with in Vietnam, and within ten years three of the six had committed suicide," he says with sadness. Even more disheartening was the loss of his closest buddy to cancer about four years ago. "That hit me hard," Joe recalls. "We'd been looking for each other for years and finally found each other on the Internet. We met the following summer in Reno. When we were alone it was like our days in the bunker in Vietnam—smoking cigars, talking and listening to country-western music."

Recently, Richart visited the traveling Vietnam Wall in Chewelah. The moment brought back haunting memories. He says, "When I walked up and looked at that, I could hear the gunfire, smell the powder and the stink, and hear the screams. I figured that the lucky ones were the ones who had their name on the wall. They don't have nightmares."

Yet Joe Richart survives, and so does his family. Thanks to VA therapy, his children over the years grew in their tolerance of his shortcomings. "They learned that my engagement with therapy meant that I was trying. I felt that they began to understand that I had been through a lot and was trying to raise them the best that I could."

And, Joe says, there's hope for the next generation. "I've got grandkids I'm going to spoil now and treat them how I should have treated my own kids."

Story by Kathleen Thamm

Pat Biggs - Continued from page 81

ordering the prime of youth and opportunity off to some ridiculous and destructive venture, only to walk away to a higher office, great wealth and the claim to fame—provided all the cover-ups pass the test of time.

Exemptions had prolonged the actual commencement of his active duty into June, 1970, though he was initially commissioned second lieutenant in the summer of 1966. By the time he reported to Vietnam in June of 1970, following graduation from law school, he was classified as a first lieutenant with nine years of longevity, though his active duty experience was limited to a few months. He also left his wife and two daughters, aged two and six weeks.

His impression of Vietnam: "I was mostly dazzled by my first experience in a foreign country outside of Canada, thousands of miles and worlds away from home, and saw all those small people, the beautiful women dressed in multi-colored sarongs, straw hats, sort of like a wild rush of Disneyland. Long Binh (Ft. Benning East) was a huge, dusty, tent-and-metal Army base that seemed to go for miles and miles, home to 35,000."

Though he had hoped to be assigned to a JAG unit, he found himself assigned as the Adjutant to the 39th Signal Battalion, in charge of administration. Seeking legal experience, he acquired the designation of Certified Defense Counsel. This credential eventually led to re-assignment to Nha Trang in Region II and eventually to Tuy Hoa as a defense counsel. There, he participated as a JAG trial lawyer in over 60 courts-martial proceedings in dozens of places involving travel over much of the central and southern regions of South Vietnam. He reports he "lost the vast majority of the judge trials but won the five jury trials."

Unlike combat veterans, Biggs was not in the presence of hostile fire though it could often be heard in the distance. His experiences of war come from being armed, flying thousands of miles over hostile territory in helicopters, and the stories told to him by clients returning from combat.

Today, Biggs rattles off Vietnamese locations like a child reciting a vocabulary lesson: Saigon, Ton San Nhut, Vung Tau, Cam Rahn Bay, Pleiku, Dalat, Phu Cat, Phang Rang, Ban Me Thuot, Can Tho, places he describes as "stops." He recalls a long helicopter flight from Saigon to Rach Gia, passing over the entire Delta, which he describes as "hundreds of miles of rice patties, pock-marked with bomb craters every few hundred feet, the entire way."

Though he did not participate in combat, he lives with the scars he believes he acquired from the entire Vietnam era ('64 to '75) experience and what followed from it, a much longer time than the 12 months he spent serving in Vietnam. "I didn't serve in a war," he says with some stress in his voice, "I participated in the Vietnam Conflict by being there for 12 months, then spent 35 years figuring out that that service was a great stigma and, if I never mentioned it to anyone, no one would ask about it." He sees history repeating itself and sees this as confirmation of the admonition of Heraclitus (535 B.C.) - "Eyes and ears are poor witnesses when the soul is barbarous."

Bronze Star, Army Commendation Medal, Vietnam Service Ribbon

Larry Scott - Continued from page 83

wounded and four men were injured so bad that they were discharged from the Army. The person who threw the grenade was never caught. We did know he was a U.S. soldier. In my mind, he was just another enemy. That night was my introduction to the horror and suffering of war, at the hands of one of our own."

While camaraderie remained fairly constant in his unit, Scott recalls one element that could wreak havoc on any soldier: drugs. "Some guys would sit there and want to smoke their joints," he says, but he didn't like the idea of anyone doing drugs and handling a rifle. "Some guys probably got shot because of it." He remembers one case in which a sergeant lost his stripes as a result of drug use. When the sarge arrived, "he had his stuff together," Scott says. "But when he left, I was higher rank than he was. I left as an A4; he was an A2. He was busted clear down because of drugs. I saw how they can ruin your life."

Another danger was Agent Orange, though Scott says he never thought he was exposed. But now he's not so sure. At age 50, he was diagnosed with cancer. "I went to the VA and told them where I'd been in Vietnam, when I was there, where I served, and they said, 'Agent Orange.'" Looking back, he admits he might have spent a short time in one of the DMZ areas that was heavily sprayed.

After Vietnam, Scott joined the Army Reserves and quickly advanced to E7. "I was promoted pretty fast because of different medals I got in Vietnam and my service time." While in the Reserves he attended drill-sergeant training and NCO academy, where he developed teaching skills. "I was able to use my experience to teach others. I was really good at it, and I had one of the best training aides available—combat experience." He could tell a trainee about actual combat situations, because he knew firsthand.

Though he had a successful transition from active to Reserve duty, Scott experienced problems as a civilian. One was divorce. Of his marriage he says, "My wife always felt I ran it like a drill instructor. She told me I had Vietnam stress syndrome, so I went and had myself tested, and they said it was a very mild case." But Scott and his wife could not find a compromise and concluded that divorce was the only option.

A related problem was his social life. "When you come back from a war," he says, "you expect to come back to what you were doing and the life you had when you went in." Sadly, that wasn't the case. Upon returning, he says, "My buddies were married or moved, and there was nobody I could really run around with like I did before. The guys still there were druggies or whatever, and that wasn't my bag."

To fill his time, he went back to his pre-war job at a supermarket chain, which led to another problem. He worked the night shift, but the store didn't like his performance. "They said I wasn't adjusting, and they fired me." Scott took his case to the VA, for violation of reemployment rights of a veteran, and he won. The supermarket paid him for time lost, and he was offered a reinstatement. But he declined and moved on.

Not long after Vietnam, Larry Scott moved to Spokane "to get a new start in life someplace else." He's found friends among the vets in the area, but he doesn't often speak of his military service. He says he doesn't wear anything, like a cap or a jacket, to indicate he's a Vietnam vet. "I don't know why, but I just wear the ribbon," he says. He figures if other Vietnam vets see the ribbon, they'll know.

"Yeah, I don't have to say it; they can see it."

Bronze Star, Vietnam Campaign Medal, Vietnam Defense Medal, Army Good Conduct Medal, Army Reserve Achievement Medal, National Defense Medal

---

Phil White - Continued from page 85

he says, 'I don't tolerate any smoking of dope, I don't tolerate any taking of dope. If I see you, I'll shoot you, and you'll just be a casualty.' I believed him." The CO reasoned that high or stoned soldiers could not keep each other out of danger. White agreed and avoided drugs of any kind.

Phil White will never forget December 17, 1969. "That date for me is in infamy," he says, "and I do celebrate it every year, my second birth date."

His unit had been working a night perimeter in the bush near Chu Lai. White had just completed a midnight watch, and he lay asleep on the ground. Suddenly the area exploded with the deafening noise of battle. "The Vietnamese Special Forces attacked us," White explains. "They were throwing grenades, charges, and mortars. One of my compatriots got a mortar, and he was dead. He just didn't know it. It blew out his spine, but he was still talking. I was working on him, packing his wounds, trying to comfort him."

Meanwhile, the incoming rounds continued, and White wasn't wearing his helmet. "Because it was the middle of the night and it was raining, I had used my helmet as a pillow to keep my head out of the mud. A grenade hit my head, bounced off, and blew up."

Because of its proximity when exploding, the grenade did considerable damage, and White's injury forced him out of combat. "I was hospitalized for 17 months," he says. During that time he was encouraged to talk about the injury, the combat, the pain. "I was one of the fortunate few to go through that process and get rid of most of the pain and anger and turmoil."

Sadly, White suffered meningitis due to the injury. While at the hospital in Japan, he lapsed into a coma, and his parents flew there to say goodbye. But he regained consciousness, and he and his father flew together back to San Diego.

That's where he endured the worst indignity of all.

Recalling the incident, he says, "We landed in San Francisco right next to Travis Air Force Base. Back in the '60s and '70s, they didn't have the big concourses like they do now. You got off the plane and walked across the runway. They unloaded everybody who was on a stretcher, then put them into ambulances. At that time they had a barricade around the area, but protestors broke down a barrier and came up and spit on us guys that were on the stretchers."

In his semi-conscious state, White couldn't see and could barely hear. Still, he realized what was happening. "I was pissed," he states without apology. "We were all pissed. That still is one of the most hurtful things."

Like many Vietnam vets with similar homecoming experiences, White says he'll never forget that moment. And, he doesn't want any current soldiers to return to a similar reception. "That's why I play the pipes every opportunity I get for soldiers coming home or leaving, and I play as many funerals as I can," he says of his musical skills.

White's head injury resulted in numerous complications. Even today, he says, "I have a plate about the size of a softball in the back of my head, and scars along the side of my head. Plus, they took out a piece of brain about the size of a baseball." Upon returning to the States, he says, "I was blind, deaf and paralyzed on my right side. My vision has never come back so I do with what I got."

Fortunately, though his hearing improved. "When I first got back I was almost deaf, because the grenade had exploded so close to my head." He went to Balboa Naval Hospital in San Diego and saw "the best neurosurgeon in the country." This doctor, who also served as the presidential neurosurgeon, suggested that White should go "back to a place where I would be more familiar with my surroundings. It's one of the most intelligent things that the military has ever done for me." After returning home, he gradually recovered his hearing, and now, he says, it is exceptional. "I can hear a pin drop 100 yards or so."

Once he finished rehabilitation—which included learning how to walk and talk again—White decided to go back to college, where he faced an immediate stumbling block with his blindness. The VA hired note-takers for him, but White didn't find them helpful. Eventually, he decided against higher education.

But that doesn't mean he quit learning. "I started listening to a lot of books," he says. "I educated myself. When I was rehabilitated to learn how to speak, one of my instructors said the most important thing was to have a huge vocabulary. Then nobody can say that because of your disability you are illiterate. I took that to heart."

Besides his brain injury, another problem plagues this soldier: Agent Orange. But he sees it with an optimistic attitude. "I get tumors periodically, nothing severe. They just cut them out; it's not a big deal. You just got to keep on keeping on. Some days are really, really good and some days are really, really bad. Most of them maybe are in between."

White's military awards include the Army Commendation with Valor and the Purple Heart. He belongs to the Purple Heart Association, and he serves as an officer in the VFW. At meetings, he and the others don't often talk of combat and injuries and rehab. Instead, he says, "We hang around, commiserate, have a few beers. It is just kind of a support. You know, Joe Blow meets, talks about something, usually family stuff." He values their simple camaraderie.

White plays bagpipes whenever he's called upon—including at the annual Veteran's Day ceremony in Spokane. The strains of "Amazing Grace" flow from his pipes toward the Bronze Soldier at the Vietnam Veterans Memorial in Riverfront Park. For the past 15 years, White has participated in the ceremony, and he hopes to continue the tradition so that the generations following will also remember.

In spite of the trauma he experienced years ago, White is content. He says, "The government has given me a comfortable lifestyle. I don't live luxuriously, but I'm not wanting for anything, and my medical needs are met." He says he has what's necessary to "make me a more productive person in society. I do my VFW meetings, and I can do other things that I want. I have nothing but good things to say about the VA, because they have treated me very well over the years."

He looks back on his time in Vietnam with a mixture of emotions. "Those who missed combat are fortunate in a way—and they are unfortunate in a way," he asserts, "because you never, will ever, ever have a life experience like that again."

Ralph Noll - Continued from page 87

settle down to a regular life. He never recovered what he lost. He was surprised to learn on his return that civilians accused Vietnam veterans of terrible crimes. Employers would not hire them. Protestors spit on them and yelled obscenities. He was scum. Over the years he experienced two broken marriages. He is alienated from his children and has had fifty-two jobs in twenty-five years. The emotional and physical pain is still a part of his everyday life.

Story by Olivia Wegis

Vietnam Service Medal

MedEvac is coming in and taking my buddy; but they left me because I wasn't bleeding." Still, he'd been injured, too, and he would deal with pain throughout the remainder of his tour and in the years that followed.

After months in Vietnam, Montgomery began experiencing fear—sometimes with good reason, sometimes not. "I would pull extra guard duty just so I wouldn't have to be out in the open walking," he recalls. "I was afraid for me and my friends, my fellow soldiers being shot."

Once, while in the chow line, he heard gunfire overhead. "The mortar tube went POOF, PHEW, PHEW! three times, and chills went down my spine. I had this tray of food, and I threw it and dropped everything." At the time, he wasn't carrying his M-16, so he dashed to one of the bunkers. Grabbing a weapon, he scanned the horizon for the enemy. "My eyes went right to where they were, three of them, about 250 yards away."

He fired three rounds. "I saw one go down and I thought, 'Oh no, I hit him.' I didn't want to hurt anybody, kill anybody, I never did. I don't like war. It didn't feel good at all."

In a quiet voice, he remembers the moment and says, "To this day I ask myself, Why me? Why was I the only one that returned fire?"

The incident proved to be a tipping point for Montgomery. "That's when I flipped out. They couldn't get me to go out on the worksites. Physically, I wasn't able to do any lifting, so I quit. I gave up."

As a result, he yielded to the temptation of marijuana, and his superiors suspected him of it. "The company commander comes up to me and says, 'I hear you've been indulging in certain unspeakable activities.' I didn't laugh. I was petrified."

Montgomery feared he'd lose rank and be arrested by MPs. But the commander softened, pointing out the dangerous combination of drugs and weapons. He finished with simple advice: "You've got to stop doing this."

Montgomery halfheartedly agreed, but it took another incident to convince him. "I was down in a village looking for pot," he remembers. As he walked along, a young woman seemed to be stalking him. She'd glance toward him and move away. He decided to investigate and ended up at a residence. "She stood by her door, and then she backed off like she wanted me to come in."

As soon as he walked inside he realized his error.

"I went in, took two steps, and whoom! Down I went, over my head with a round in the chamber. I fell into a bomb shelter or something." During the fall, he'd dropped his rifle, and he worried that the woman would shoot him with it.

"I got my head up level with the ground and looked around, and all these people were coming around. I could hear them talking. I was frightened." Then he saw his weapon on the floor to the left of the pit. He crawled out of the hole, but instead of standing he pulled a military maneuver. "I just rolled and grabbed the rifle and pointed it at the door. They all backed away. I picked up the rest of my gear and walked out."

The realization of danger made the lure of marijuana much less attractive. "I never went down in that hamlet again," he states. "I was done."

Montgomery's transition into civilian life became an ongoing process. The incident in the pit gave him nightmares, and he still endures constant pain because of the convoy accident. In addition, he's had six double hernias since Vietnam and has spent time in hospitals in the Philippines, Japan, California and Fort Lewis.

Even worse, his teenage son once caught him looking down the barrel of a rifle. "I didn't even tell anybody that I was thinking about Vietnam," he says, but the son quietly took the weapon from him, and he didn't see it again. In fact, Montgomery himself soon got rid of his other weapons, including hunting rifles.

After all, he never really wanted to kill anything.

Craig Thomas - Continued from page 91

thought I was in a car accident. Then I looked around, and I went, oh! I recognized the burnt grass and said, 'I think I got blown up.'"

Transferred to a hospital in Japan, Thomas recalls seeing several from B Company there. He also recalls the condition of his left leg. "I still had it, but it was heavily broken," and he'd lost a lot of the femur. "I was pretty reluctant to let them chop it off. They wanted to chop it off, but I said no."

After being wounded, the last thing he remembers before surgery was the wall clock, which read 10 a.m. Thankful for the early hour, Craig explains, "Had it been later in the day, I probably wouldn't have made it. The rule was that firefights get a little bit heavier in the afternoon. We had helicopters rotating 'round us because they knew there was going to be casualties."

The doctors in Japan saved his other leg, but not for long. After retiring from the service in 1969 with a full disability, Thomas discovered the doctors could not improve his condition. "I had my left leg amputated the day after Thanksgiving, 1969," he says. "I got fitted with legs and went to rehab to get rehabilitated, and then I went back to school."

Unsure of exactly what career track to choose, he moved back to his hometown. "I took advantage of a retraining program at the Community Colleges of Spokane from '70 till '74. Then I went to work for Boeing Engineers as a draftsman, followed by Gerard and Associates, as a mechanical draftsman. Then I got a job at Avista."

Craig Thomas holds little bitterness for his traumatic experience in Vietnam. "You know my basic philosophy. I've had a good life." The day he was wounded, he says, "is the only really bad or worst day, and I guess it got me out of there so it wasn't really a bad day." For his actions on October 2, 1968, Thomas received his second Purple Heart and the Silver Star for Gallantry in Action. "To this day I really don't know what actions I took to earn such a prestigious award. I felt I was only doing my job as a rifleman. However, I do feel very honored to be recognized by my fellow soldiers for my actions on that dark day."

His optimism has carried through the years, and he sees his combat experience as fundamental to the person he is today. "I don't know how I would have ended up if that hadn't happened."

Two Purple Hearts, Silver Star for Gallantry in Action

Greg L. Lambert - Continued from page 95

Looking for a fresh start, Lambert moved from Wichita, Kansas, to Auburn, Washington. There, he met fellow vets who understood his situation. One of them said, "I'm taking you to the VA hospital. You need help, son."

He was quickly diagnosed with Post Traumatic Stress Disorder. Finally, he says, someone could help. Someone could grasp the fact that there's trauma even in taking an enemy's life. While he says he'll never recover from PTSD completely, he's made good strides. He lives with his fifth wife, whom he met while living in Ione, a small town in northeast Washington. She has family nearby, and he's found his place among them. "She's the right one," he says with a smile.

Ray - Continued from page 97

The guard explained that he was under orders to shoot, and T expressed doubts that the guard would follow through. To prove his point, T dashed away, and the guard shot him in the back of the head, killing him.

"That," says Ray, "is what brought down the Congressional investigation on the Presidio. News of that went around the Presidio so quick that they almost had a riot. Overnight they hustled us out of there and the next morning we found our selves in Fort Ord."

Ray lost respect for his superiors during his time in the stockade. He says he's always been a self-governing man, uncomfortable taking orders from others. "I'm from an unusual part of the country," he says. "Independent, northern Californians—we don't need anything. We've got it all."

Perhaps that's why the military didn't work out for him. When faced with a choice, he's always taken the path of solitude over structure, nature over humankind. That's easy to do in northern California. "I'm not a people person," he declares. "Everyday I was either hunting or fishing or both. I actually preferred to hunt and fish on my own."

Gary Barton - Continued from page 101

As they neared the next port, a miscommunication about the weather caused another problem. The helicopters, all spotted on the flight deck, should have been stored below. Instead, Barton recalls, they stayed on deck, and the storm "ripped every blade off of every helicopter. When we finally got through the storm and into port, they had to crane all the helicopters off the ship and truck them away to get repaired." The ship went into dry dock and refitting began.

While Barton found deck work interesting, he'd planned to become a radioman when he enlisted. Eventually he got training and transferred from one duty station to another. "I was at nine different commands in four years," he says. "I bounced around like crazy."

In Hawaii, he was first stationed on the USS *Badger*, a fast frigate, temporarily dry-docked. After refitting, they were back out to sea.

Then Barton was transferred to a See Bee unit on Ford Island. "The Arizona Memorial in next to the island," he points out. "It was a great reminder of why we were there." And a year later he transferred to the

USS *Ponchatoula*, a refueling ship, and experienced yet another unexpected incident. A violent storm at sea found him on duty and reluctantly responsible for the massive cleanup that followed.

During his final five months, he came full circle, working again as a deckhand—but this time on a tugboat. His job involved learning all the steps to hooking the tug to a ship and maintaining the lines while entering and departing from port.

In spite of the problems and potential dangers, Gary Barton benefited from his years in the Navy. "They taught me how to work for a living," he declares.

Besides, he had the opportunity to leave his home and see the world.

Shane Richter - Continued from page 103

reach him. The next thing I knew I heard his name on the news and raced home to tell my wife that Joe was in trouble."

With a shake of his head, Richter says, "Three days after that we found out he had committed suicide."

The news hit Richter like a blow to the gut, and he spent years grieving. But now he sees the event in a different light. "I've grown a little, and the fact that he died is sad, but it doesn't erase the good times. Joe was a real friend."

In spite of this sorrow, Richter sees his military service as a good experience. "In my whole six years the morale was positive," he states. "Just my luck: I served with a great bunch of guys who worked together well, got along well, and played together well."

April Bresgal - Continued from page 107

Sexual harassment, too, was part of her day, most often from guys she didn't work with. Comments about how she might look out of uniform and uninvited sexual advances were obstacles she had to dodge. She felt fortunate in that it never went further than that.

"There was no good way to confront the ones who wouldn't quit when I asked them to," she says. "You were damned if you complained, and damned if you didn't. Ostracized for getting some guy in trouble or stuck with just putting up with it. Putting up with it was usually easier."

While "I won't go out with you because I don't date co-workers" was her usual answer to requests for date, the truth was that Bresgal was gay and not interested in dating men, co-workers or not. This, of course, became her major on-going problem. As a source of stress, it did not ever go away. It only got worse.

When she had enlisted the first time, back in 1974, she says, "I decided that I was going to live my life within my own expectations of myself as a gay person, which meant I was not going entirely in the closet." However, the compromises began that first day. Reading over the enlistment contract, she realized she was going to have to lie. 'Have you ever engaged in homosexual activities?' was right there next to 'Have you ever been a felon?' She says that "I understood that answering 'no' to that question was required if I wanted to enlist and do something with my life, so I did. That was painful to me. I don't like to lie."

It became more and more difficult to relax and live her life. In the beginning, she had been open with her co-workers about her relationships. But as time went on, she earned promotions and began to make more money. As she was transferred to new bases and new assignments, she befriended fewer and fewer of her co-workers. There began to be too much to lose.

After four years she was offered the opportunity to re-enlist. She loved her job, her service, and her standard of living, but she realized she could not reenlist. "As a gay person, it was too dangerous. I could not make a life commitment to the Air Force when they could throw me out without a penny at any time because of my sexual orientation."

She separated from the Air Force and tried her hand at college again. As she had hoped, it was much easier this time, and she was very successful in school. However, after a couple years, she decided she needed a part-time job and she missed the service. So, she enlisted in the Washington Air National Guard.

Looking back, she remembers a later re-enlistment after President Clinton instituted the so-called "Don't Ask, Don't Tell" policy. "Now" she says, "that question is not on the contract anymore. That was such a relief to me." She still didn't feel comfortable enough to come out to the guys she worked with, but, she says, "It was one less lie."

She retired after 20 years total service in 2001, and she says, "I feel good about my service to my country. We need the armed forces. We need people who are willing to fight and die because that is the world we live in today. I wish it wasn't true, but it is. I am one of the people willing and able to do that."

Her only regret is that she was not allowed to be open about her sexual orientation and continue her service as an active military member. "It was really difficult to discourage friendships and avoid certain conversations with people I know liked and cared about me. I think some guys misunderstood and were hurt by the distance I kept. That was sad. And, as a result, I have only a couple of friendships left from those 20 years of service."

Story by April Bresgal

Air Force Meritorious Service Medal, Washington State Air National Guard Commendation Medal, Washington State Air National Guard Emergency Service Ribbon

Seth Van Eyck - Continued from page 109

Van Eyck's unit faced frequent dangers in Iraq, and he sustained numerous injuries during his time in country. "The first IED that I hit tore up my knee and my back pretty bad," he says, but he didn't immediately realize the extent of his problems. In 2008, he discovered "a piece of metal coming out of my armpit that I didn't even know had been there." What's more, "My brain got knocked around inside my head, and at some point I was told I'd had a trauma-induced stroke."

Despite these problems, he wasn't shipped out of Iraq until he started having nightmares.

That's when the brass decided he needed some rest. "I was diagnosed with extreme posttraumatic stress disorder and traumatic brain injury. I also had a blown-out eardrum, torn cartilage in my knee, and problems with a disk in my low back."

When he returned to the States, he says he tried drugs: "uppers, downers and sidewayers. But after awhile I got tired of looking at my life as a movie like everything was going on behind glass." So he stopped the medications except for occasional painkillers, which will always be needed. "They told me I'm going to be in pain for the rest of my life, because it is degenerating into arthritis. I get extremely bad headaches where, if I could, I would take a drill and drill a hole into my head."

Obviously, life isn't easy for Van Eyck. "I forget things, I forget words, I get really, really depressed. I go through cycles where I'm depressed and then I'm just back up on Cloud Nine with manic episodes. My self-esteem is in the toilet because I feel like a coward. I left my men and came home. I've got problems; but you know, everybody has problems, so I have a hard time dealing with that."

He blames himself for the loss of some in his unit. "I was up on the gun on my truck, and the IED detonated and killed one of my men and wounded six. Having seven guys taken out in one day, that was half our strength; and I never recovered from that. I feel like it was my fault." He believes if he'd been on the ground instead of at the gun, someone else would've been spared.

Though he has no more tears for that event, he lives with a deep sorrow. Trying to understand a Higher Power has helped. "I have my own relationship with God," he says, "but I can't wrap my head around God wanting us all to grab hold of all these ideals and give these men so much control, the kind of control that leads us to go off to other places and kill each other. I can't see where that would be part of His plan."

Instead, Seth Van Eyck has established his own list of ideals. "I think He wants us all to be kind and nice to each other. If you have a good, honest heart, maybe He will see you through things and maybe He will be there to help you when you need it."